D1253347

The Critique of Modernity
Theological Reflections
on Contemporary Culture

JULIAN N. HARTT

RAY L. HART

ROBERT P. SCHARLEMANN

The
Critique
of
Modernity

Theological Reflections
on
Contemporary Culture

UNIVERSITY PRESS OF VIRGINIA
Charlottesville

THE UNIVERSITY PRESS OF VIRGINIA
Copyright © 1986 by the Rector and Visitors
of the University of Virginia

First published 1986

Library of Congress Cataloging-in-Publication Data

Hartt, Julian Norris.
  The critique of modernity.

  Contents: The pathos of community in contemporary
culture / Julian N. Hartt—The dialectic of home
and homelessness : religion, nature, and home / Ray L.
Hart—The forgotten self and the forgotten divine /
Robert P. Scharlemann.
  1. Christianity and culture. 2. Individuality.
I. Hart, Ray L. II. Scharlemann, Robert P.
III. Title.
BR115.C8H385 1986   261   86-13251
ISBN 0-8139-1118-4

Printed in the United States of America

Contents

JULIAN N. HARTT
Introduction

THESE VIRGINIA LECTURES on Individual and Society were given
during the first week of March 1984. The lecturers were Ray
Hart, Professor of Religious Studies, University of Montana;
Julian Hartt, Kenan Professor emeritus of Religious Studies,
University of Virginia; and Robert Scharlemann, Common-
wealth Professor of Religious Studies, University of Virginia.
The lectureship is sponsored by the Committee on Comparative
Study of Individual and Society and by the Center for Advanced
Studies, University of Virginia.

The general title of this series was "The Critique of Modernity:
Theological Reflections on Contemporary Culture." The lecturers were not asked to work with themes common to their several
approaches. Nevertheless, such themes emerge in their treat-
ments of the critique of modernity. Of these none is more important, and clearly none closer to the constitutive concerns of the
committee, than the conviction that the reality and worth of the
individual are seriously compromised by modern doctrines concerning the relationship of self to society. It does not follow, and
it may not be the case, that a return to some hitherto established
truth is thus indicated. A consensus on that does not emerge in
the papers presented in this series.

I

Religious commentary on society and culture is not a modern
phenomenon. The prophets in ancient Israel made an appraisal
of their cultural environment that has many elements of a critique in the sense in which that work is commonly used today.
They found little to commend, much to excoriate, in the life,
corporate and individual, of the chosen people. In their view
Israel, the covenant community, is guilty of apostasy. The reg-
nant piety and morals are offense to the Lord, who is the author
and sustainer of the covenant. Therefore the chosen people can
expect nothing but dire affliction until they return to the ethical
religious life for which God has called them and apart from which
they have no real life. Then in the Christian context one thinks

INTRODUCTION

of St. Paul's critique of the moral degradation of life in Roman society; then of the fulminations of the church fathers against the immoralities and religious practices of the pagan world. Some of this negativism persists in St. Augustine's appraisal of the culture of the Roman Empire; but he probes for the foundations in being and history of the City of Man. He looks, that is, for the ontological-theological roots of human society, not just of Rome. His *City of God*, therefore, is a critique profounder and more sophisticated than conventional religious appraisals of culture, whether they are positive or negative. Augustine's critique, thus, is intended to uncover the enduring realities of human community. As for therapy, he has a very slight investment in symptomatic relief. Since the roots of the distortion of human existence are deep in history and being, their healing must lie beyond human powers.

The distinction between a conventional and a radical critique of culture has an enduring significance, a fact amply illustrated by American society past and present. Conventional religious critiques largely tend to be moralistic both in tone and in substance. They hold that America is afflicted with formidable problems both at home and abroad because there has been a wholesale departure from moral rules and dispositions presumptively divine in their provenance and sanctions. Thus the avowals of the leaders of the Moral Majority. Similar convictions are expressed by neoconservatives whether or not they share any of the theological principles of fundamentalist preachers. They too believe that America's providential institutions have been jettisoned or deeply compromised by the liberal apostasy. Accordingly, the recovery of health for the body politic demands a return to the system of values embedded in the major institutions of American life: school, family, church, market place and labor force, as they existed before liberal tampering with them. Today the political welkin rings with the cry, Return to traditional values! These are all but universally identified as "Judeo-Christian."

The prevailing disposition today is to think of radical critiques of culture as Marxist in inspiration if not in substantive policies. "Revolutionary" has the same resonance. "Leftist" powerfully suggests an inclination—if not a diabolically complete agenda—for dismantling the prime institutions and their philosophical backing, replacing them with dreadful modern novelties of social institution and worldview.

Conflicts between conservative and radical critiques of culture include a persistent quarrel over "humanism" and "humanistic." One side uses "humanistic" as a pejorative, rendering it virtually synonymous with "atheistic," as though to be in favor of the *human* is ipso facto to be against the *divine*. So it is said that humanists have banished God from the public schools. Preachers who say this probably do not have in mind a metaphysical-historical event comparable to the expulsion of Adam and Eve from Eden. A deity who could be manhandled by a Deweyite humanist is hardly worth the effort. Nor could his metaphysical fortunes be repaired by Constitutional amendments.

The other side features endless disputes over whose humanism is the real thing. Marxists, Freudians, existentialists, pragmatists, all enter their claims and reject the credentials of the competitors. So it is not surprising that conservative Christians should want to cry havoc on all their houses and let loose the word of God against them all. But it was not very long ago when other voices were confidently bespeaking the interests of a *Christian* humanism; voices Protestant and Catholic. Thinkers as different both from conventional figures and from each other as Jacques Maritain and Paul Tillich come to mind. Both of them had deep reservations about modern institutions regarded as precious and providential by conventional critics. Neither Tillich nor Maritain proposed or defended a massive return to a blessed human condition realized in a long-lost and all-but-forgotten era.

The distinction between conventional and radical religious critiques of culture is not the only one to be drawn. The second one I propose here may seem to be invidious and prejudicial to the interests of the conservative side. This is the distinction between theologians and preachers. Perhaps its offensiveness can be reduced by making it general in application, thus assuring injury to both parties. Such is the demand of justice if not of truth.

There was a time when this distinction would not have made sense. The important theological work was then done by preachers in their pulpits, not by professors in their endowed chairs. One thinks of Jonathan Edwards in the eighteenth century and of Horace Bushnell in the nineteenth. In the meantime *preacher* has come to be very largely identified as a Protestant phenomenon. Catholic priests and Jewish rabbis are rarely so identified, and with some reason: neither priest nor rabbi has the responsibility for delivering the "word" as the centerpiece if not the raison d'être of stated religious observance.

Taken on the conventional understanding, the preacher is not a professional thinker either in respect of theological matters or of any others. It has in fact been a long time since a man of the pulpit made an enduring contribution to the intellectual life of religion or to intellectual life more generally. The modern understanding of the task of the preacher is that he should remind his people of what they are already supposed to know (= believe). It is not up to the preacher to add novel items to the inventories of things known and knowable. He is presumed to be the monitor and administrator of knowledge that requires action in the social world. Christian behavior, the Christian life, is the end in view of preaching in the modern conception. Intellectual novelties, philosophic depth, scientific sophistication: these are not widely or passionately sought by or from the Protestant pulpit. They would not be ecstatically received if they were produced by the preacher.

These generalizations about the contemporary Protestant preacher in the church largely hold for secular preaching in the general society. I do not mean by secular preaching the performances of the ordained clergyman at the Kiwanis Club or at national political conventions. The fact is that the American politician is expected to be something of a preacher whether or not he refers to the presidential office as a "bully pulpit." As a rhetorician the politician appeals to things taken for granted by his audience, or that ought to be taken for granted. The church preacher waves the bible, the politician the flag or other conventional symbols, verbal and nonverbal, of the blessed common life. He is not expected to propound philosophical or scientific novelties or lead the flock into the deep waters of metaphysical speculation. He appeals to traditions of the nation and claims that they are best served by his party and his policies. He may claim that he has the moral principles and the vision for a wonderful enlargement of life for the nation, perhaps even for the world (human rights, a world safe for democracy, the right of self-determination, free enterprise for all, etc.). But as preacher he does not deliberately propose things hard to understand. His hearers may claim not to grasp how *he* can stand for what he claims or how, upon being elected, he could possibly turn society in the direction he advocates as desirable. But he would sooner bite off his tongue than weave mystical or metaphysical profundities into his public discourse.

Moreover just as the church preacher in contemporary society is not expected to enrich the intellectual life of the congregation, so also the secular preachers add little or nothing to the store of political philosophy. They are not professional thinkers, they are professional talkers. Of course this does not rule out the possibility of one being able to factor real insight into one's discourse, particularly insight into the political process; any more than the life of the church renders impossible the appearance in it of a preacher of deep insight into human existence and into the moral configurations of the social world environing the church. Even so as preacher, either church or secular, his first and overriding responsibility is not to add to the philosophical capital of the institution he serves as a professional. It has been a long time since a preacher in either institution, church or civil state, has powerfully stimulated or otherwise enriched reflection on the doctrinal foundations of the institution.

II

A brief sketch of persisting species of theological critiques of culture may be useful here. This is not intended to function as a set of slots to receive and retain the views of the three lecturers in this series. Interest in it should hardly run beyond discerning affinities linking these views with perennial types of theological critiques.

(1) Using the bible as an inerrant and infallible fount of wisdom and truth, theologians have delineated the ways in which culture fails to fulfill the divine demands for righteousness in self and society. Such a critical weapon has two barrels: one loaded to attack false teaching, the other to expose immoralities gross and subtle. Augustine fired both barrels: there are false teachings inside and outside the church; but he would not have bothered with them in such persistence and vigor had he thought they were capable of intellectual mischief only. In his view the prime evil in heresy is its ability to divide the church, thereby threatening to make *Catholic* a fractional and factional institution, spreading its divisive gospel abroad into civil society. So while the heresiarch may have a character morally unimpeachable, his doctrine and his zeal in promulgating it threaten to destroy the spiritual-ethical unity of the community.

Today the most visible and audible religious critique is much like this first type. If its protagonists were *theologically* serious, they would offer a reasoned defense of the doctrine of scriptural inerrancy and infallibility; that doctrine itself is not scriptural. This they rarely do. The truth of the doctrine is presupposed in

xi

order to do the main work. That is to attack the failure to realize scriptural righteousness, construed legalistically, as God's demands upon self and society. That failure is not represented as universal. To the contrary, some people are self-recognized as fit and ready to join the holy communion of saints on earth and in heaven.

The essays presented here are clearly hostile to this type of critique. None of them regards it as theologically serious. All of them concede, nonetheless, that it is a vexatiously striking religious-cultural phenomenon, a pathological condition not to be ignored.

Using a philosophical-metaphysical system, theologians have sought to determine where the contemporary culture is in the grand process of history. Since the middle of the nineteenth century the two most influential forms of this type have been the Hegelian and the personalist. In America the personalist form has had the larger following and the larger influence. Much more obviously and straightforwardly the personalist critique presses for an evaluation of the moral value of contemporary institutions, given the infinite worth of persons in the sight of God and enlightened humanity. The influence of this view in the rise and triumphs of the Social Gospel was immense.

None of the essays in this series can be understood as the second type; none, that is, presupposes the truth of a philosophical system. On the other hand none is hostile to an ethical appraisal of contemporary societal structures. In fact each grants that such an appraisal must be part of a theological critique and not an afterthought. But to respond to such questions as What does it mean to be a person, a realized self? none of them turns to a philosophical system. The main reason for this is the contemporary philosophical situation, mentioned below.

Using a philosophical analytic, theologians assess the intelligibility and credibility of the Christian message in and for a secularized society. The waning of the star of metaphysics in contemporary philosophy has given great impetus to the development of theological critiques in this third mode. It has three main lines: (a) The analytic of logical positivism. At best this was a slender reed for theological purposes. That this was so was discovered at just about the time philosophers pronounced it inadequate for their own purposes. (b) The analytic of phenomenology. With this instrument theologians probe for the social-historical forces at work in the surface realities of the contemporary life. The surfaces are bound to be misleading as, say, neurotic formations of personality are misleading though not intentionally so. Thus moralistic judgments of self and society are part of the surface realities requiring interpretation. Accordingly the Moral Majority is important as a phenomenon to be understood but not as an epitomization of the Christian message or as a possibility for an authentic Christian existence. (c) The analytic of hermeneutics. Here theologians employ principles of interpretation first of texts and thereafter of language more generally; language understood as the paramount human reality, if not as the only reality open to human discernment and human actualization. Such principles of interpretation are suitable not just for religious texts and religious language but are universally valid. Religious thinkers in fact were among the earliest in the Western World to develop theories about the limits and potencies of language. They used methods and principles appropriate for all manner of texts and linguistic forms, for example the distinction between literal and symbolic discourse.

The third essay (Scharlemann) in this series is the closest to this last mode of critique. For that purpose the philosopher, the pioneer figure, is Heidegger. The second essay (Hart) also shows a marked affinity for linguistic analysis in the third mode. However, deeply sympathetic to Goethe's philosophical views, Hart looks for language's engagement with the being of man, nature, and God.

Working from the assumption that the bible reveals "a strange new world" alternative to every and any merely human worldview or philosophy of life, theologians use its truths, above all available in the master images of scripture, to appraise the cultural and personal achievements of the contemporary world. Here the bible is not regarded as science-before-science or as a volume of moral rules; rather, it is held to be source of imaginational potencies necessary for the interpretation of existence, history, and cosmos. But, again, interpretation is incomparably more than an intellectual exercise; rather, it is the divinely sustained response to revelation. Interpretation so construed entails a pattern of human activity understood as mandated by the absolutely authoritative disclosure of God's being as righteous will, creative and redemptive. So one of the imperial images of the bible is covenant, the act of God in which the normative community is established. There the ultimate destiny of humankind altogether is prefigured. Given the creation and persistence of the normative

INTRODUCTION

community, the first law of Christian existence becomes faithfulness. Faithfulness as a disposition to act in certain ways rather than as acceptance of certain articles of belief. Faith in that latter sense is not eliminated; it is placed in a role secondary to faith in the former sense.

This sort of theological platform has affinities with the critique mounted by the prophets in ancient Israel. Faithlessness, apostasy, breach of covenant: the consequences of dereliction so fundamental and inclusive are everywhere discernible—to the eyes of faith. The social system is committed to the worship of false gods; the system, not just individuals here and there or a social class. And above all, the social system draped and disguised with its religiosity: Christendom is the enemy of authentic Christianity. That is to say, culture-religion, promiscuous in its use of traditional Christian symbols and profligate in the advertisement of its adherence to spiritual values, is the greatest of all stumbling blocks in the way of authentic Christian faith and life. For it is fatally easy to be an "accommodation" Christian, one adept in using belief and symbol and community to sanctify self-love and self-aggrandizement. But to be a real Christian is infinitely hard. The demand to take up one's cross and follow Christ is not an invitation to a soiree or a picnic. As the world counts and applauds success, the rewards of authentic faith are painfully thin, bony, and fragile.

The twentieth-century theologian most easily identified with a critique of this order was Karl Barth. In the early part of his extraordinarily productive career, specifically in the second edition of his _Commentary on the Epistle to the Romans_, Barth nearly outdoes Kierkegaard's _Attack on Christendom_. Barth found little in modern Western culture to love, honor and obey as fulfilling God's demand for righteousness. Again, the social-cultural system is idolatrous, created in man's image for man's aggrandizement. He did not claim that every element of the system is as filthy rags in the sight of God. But as in ancient Israel so now: conventional piety claims divine ratification of the existing state of affairs. The present age is a temple dedicated to the worship of false gods.

The fourth mode of theological critique evinces a marked tension with American piety both church and secular. Once again the currents of Christian chauvinism course strongly through the nation. Once again church pulpit and political rostrum preach that Americans are the truly chosen people and the

xiv

Republic is the last best hope of earth. Surely such sentiments are piteously vulnerable to attack from this position.

In fact, however, this fourth critique is not a major feature of the current scene; nor has it been since Reinhold Niebuhr was in his prime. What accounts for this? Perhaps this kind of critique strikes people as too much like hellfire-damnation preaching. Or perhaps such an appraisal deals too harshly with sacred sentiments and institutions. Or it is taken to be fundamentalism in disguise because of its emphasis on the Word of God. (In fact fundamentalists have been severely critical of it.)

There is another kind of explanation for the lack of potency in this mode in the current scene. It is an explanation that may have more attraction for theologians than for the general public, a risk worth running nevertheless. Perhaps, that is, this critique does not offer a sufficiently radical evaluation of modern individualism. To put it in loaded terms, there is too much Kierkegaard in it, too much of existentialist elevation of the individual at the expense of that splendid solitary's essential relatedness to others. To grant the seriousness of this attack does not properly entail a rejection of Heidegger's appropriation of such Kierkegaardian motifs as the concept of Dread (Angst). Nor is it to slight Heidegger's account of authentic (personal) existence and of the inauthenticities of the "Everyday" world in which self-responsibility is glossed in favor of anonymity.

I have just said that such a response to this fourth mode of theological critique is likely to hold more interest for theologians than for anyone else. Recent events in the Roman Catholic world may make one wonder whether that is true. There seems to be a wide interest in the quarrels over liberation theology in the Roman Catholic church, for instance. There liberation theology is under heavy fire for incorporating Marxist social analysis with its interpretation of the Christian Gospel. Two things stand out in that indictment: one, Marxist social thought is deemed to be incorrigibly materialistic in one or more senses; two, the class struggle is accepted as an implacable given of modern society, from which the liberationists draw the inference that authentic Christian witness must take the side of the downtrodden masses.

In an odd way this situation points to the crux of modernity (—"crux" as in crucifixion). Social theory, Marxist and non-Marxist, tends to view the individual as a "product," a creature, of the sociocultural environment. Popular doctrine tends as strongly to be individualistic, viewing society as an aggregate of self-determining units. The fourth mode of theological critique sheds little light on this conflict. It is fine to warn both parties about the danger of idolatry, that is of false absolutes. It is generally the other side which is guilty of such a thing. That is one of the reasons it is hard to make the doctrine of Original Sin popular; there is no practical advantage confessing that we have all gone astray; the practical advantage is in discovering that one's opponents have gone further astray.

None of the essays presented here displays a clear affinity for the fourth mode of theological critique. To this extent at least these essays illustrate the failure of the Barthian critique of culture to establish a firm beachhead on the American front.

III

As the concluding section of this introduction I venture a somewhat more systematic account of the approaches to the theological critique taken by the three lecturers. Thus I exercise the right of the last word but must accept also its responsibilities. There is a measure of justice in this because by the luck of the draw I was required to have the first word. In what follows I hope that I have not grievously abused my less-than-monarchical prerogatives.

In the first essay Hartt considers misgivings about modernity very different from those prosecuted by the great "masters of suspicion," Marx, Nietzsche, and Freud. The difference is not simply the fact that those masters were professional thinkers, two of them philosophers; whereas the critique Hartt is interested in emanates from "the grass roots." There is little to be gained, for that matter, from either claiming or implying that the grass roots are incapable of producing philosophical profundities. A fair number of informed people would argue that Lincoln's grasp of the essentials of democracy was superior to Wilson's, though the latter was the only academic political philosopher to have served as president of this country. The prime difference between the critiques offered by the masters of suspicion and the grass-roots critique is to be found in the heavy commitment of the latter to certain moral values, traditional in and for America, as the wedge if not the fulcrum of attack on the corporation. Marx, Nietzsche, and Freud all construed conventional morality if not moral value as such as a systematic illusion, as part, that is, of the fabric of "false consciousness." This is not at all to say that they were devoid of moral sentiments or oblivious to moral concerns. Rather, they saw no reason to isolate the moral dimension of modern life from the inherent inclusive structure of the social world, that, again, being a false consciousness. Marx's profound reluctance to talk about justice did not spring from a conviction that it was unreal or unimportant. In his view "justice" was tainted with social-reformist idealism, an attitude fully prepared, indeed predisposed, to settle for halfway measures in restructuring the social order. Moreover, social idealism was incurably predisposed to a voluntaristic rationalistic doctrine of human being according to which the creation of a humane social order must wait upon the education and orchestration of men of good will; which is to say that a *moral* revolution is postulated as a necessary condition for rational and humane social-economic-political revolution. For Marx that would be a catastrophic triumph of class-serving ideology.

In Hartt's view the grass-roots critique of modernity has a primary focus on *covenant* as the moral heart of community. In turn the heart of covenant is promise, the self-involving performative (verbal gesture) in which a person freely binds herself or himself to another person for the sake of a good richer than either of them taken in isolation from each other or taken aggregatively. Thus an act in which the other is esteemed as irreplaceably valuable in his or her own right. Thus a situation, a relationship, in which quid-pro-quo calculations are at best ancillary to a moral-spiritual communion (ethical unity).

What Hartt calls the corporation achieved a monumental transformation of covenant-promise through the development of the *contract*, itself a triumph of calculative rationality. Surely that feature of large-scale institutions by itself did not entail the enormous weight given to impersonality in the grass-roots critique of modernity. Presumably what Hartt meant to say in this connection is that contract, the amoral heart of the corporation, has no concern for the concrete individuality of the persons subscribing to it as the instrument for the furtherance of material ends. It is not clear why there should be such a concern; economic instruments are generally not viewed or intended to be whole-souled humanistic devices bearing on the human good as such, whatever that might be. A contract has a limited goal; and it proposes limited means for the attainment of that goal; and it recognizes limited penalties for its capricious abrogation. Nonetheless, it is to be admitted that contract appears in modernity as a powerful metaphor expressing connections once deemed profoundly moral but now steeped in language and material practice that are moral only in appearance, if that, not in reality.

Hartt does not identify the conflict between covenant-community and corporation as a dialectical tension. As Ray Hart delineates the interrelationships of home and homelessness, the notion of such a tension is indispensable for understanding them. In his view religion is inescapably involved with that tension, in part because religion itself is dialectical: it is both a binding and a setting free. Here Hart makes use of etymological derivations: "religion" from the Latin *ligare* (= to bind); *religare* (= to unbind, untie). So there is a conservative pole in religion: a powerful inclination to hold time and human energy in bondage to immutable principle and archaic rite. But there is also the progressive (for want of a better word for it) pole: a powerful inclination to choose adventure over security, creativity rather than tradition, the frontier rather than the established society. It is futile to say which pole constitutes "real" or "true" religion. (Which is the "true" activity of the heart, systole or diastole?) Modernity tends to ignore this dialectical tension in and of religion. That makes it easier to construe religion per se as reactionary and secularism as progressive, religion as antihumanistic, secularism as the long-delayed liberation of the human spirit from the dead hand of the past.

As Hart sees it, this aspect of modernity has a close connection with another one. That is a fixation upon *historicity* as a defining characteristic of human being. Thereby the real situation of human being in nature is obscured.

It is not hard to see how this "de-naturing" of human existence came about. Consider (a) the modern scientific-philosophical view of nature. And (b) the immense amplification of scientific-logical capabilities for exploiting the natural environment. Given these modern doctrines and policies, how or why should we look upon nature as *home*? Only a philosopher would attempt that; at that, only a philosopher who had serious reservations about the modern scientific view of nature as an order of things governed wholly by mechanical laws.

Goethe was such a philosopher. He was a powerful and impassioned critic of Newtonian science, and of traditional Christian theology. Hart makes sustained use of Goethe. He finds in this great artist and thinker important clues for a fresh re-situating (re-ligation) of human being in and with nature. In this connection Hart raises a question rarely considered by Christian theologians: Could the ultimate extinction of the human species be part of the cosmic-divine scheme of things entire?

It is not surprising that Christian theologians and preachers should find such a notion repellent. The extinction of a considerable part of the human community has long been regarded in some Christian quarters as certain and as certainly desirable. But an irreversible death of the entire human stock? Unthinkable!—Nor is it surprising that many people untutored by theologians and preachers should find the notion unsettling. For a "postmodern" possibility is the self-destruction of the species; not by design but by accident; not as something intended but as something ineluctably consequent upon things intended. Other natural species have perished in cosmic accidents, such as a very large meteorite crashing into this planet. But the destruction of *homo sapiens* might come about as a *historical* accident, that is, as the unintended result of putatively rational decisions. Unintended but not unconsidered.

Hart does not carry the unsettling question quite this far in quite this direction. He believes it demands a reassessment of modern prepossessions about individuality. These modern views of self and society are strongly reinforced by conventional Christianity. The modern spirit quite overcame Enlightenment ambiguities in the understanding of man's place in nature, and came to see the ego's drive for power and pelf in this world and the dream of peace in the world to come, if any, as provisions of nature and nature's God, if any. What nature thus ordains let neither man nor God deny.

Hartt sees modernity as having lost sight of covenant as the moral foundation of community. Hart stresses the loss in modernity of a sustaining connection with nature as producing a marked hypertrophy of ego. Robert Scharlemann offers a diagnosis of another manifestation of amnesia in modernity: the authentic self and the authentic divine have both been forgotten, just as being itself has been forgotten.

What accounts for a pathological condition so massive and so critical? Scharlemann traces it to philosophical presumptions that have dominated Western culture for more than two millennia. One of these presumptions divides the realm of cognition altogether between concept and percept (sensation). This arbitrary division leaves no place for *understanding*. Thus deprived of the "organ" indispensable for the apprehension of being and of self-existence and of the divine, these go their several unblessed and infertile ways. Each is condemned to being, or trying to be, an *object* to and for the others. Thereby the constitutive relation between the self and the divine is lost. As one consequence of this, "God" is a being, essentially unrelated to anything else, putting in an appearance, so to speak, in and as the conclusion of a "proof" for his existence. A rather more formidable consequence for the everyday world is the lively possibility that technology will become a harsh unfeeling master of the human spirit rather than an adept servant. Such is the stuff of nightmares. Such may be the Brave New World.

Scharlemann's critique works with a large investment in language. Here again he cuts against the grain of long-regnant philosophical presumptions. Language, Scharlemann claims, is the native homeland of understanding, that unique cognitive capacity for reading signs and symbols. Thus the large significance of interpretation.

As Scharlemann sees it, interpretation is not an academic-theoretical exercise. It is the process in which existents (concrete realities) emerge in their own right of being: the autonomous self, other selves, and God (the conventional verbal sign for the divine order). Seen in this light, when Isaiah says, "Here am I! Send me" (6:8 RSV) he is not referring to an antecedently existing being, the "I." Neither is he addressing or responding to an objectlike deity, on the bizarre assumption that the two beings, Isaiah and God, have accidentally encountered each other and are trying to make something important out of that unlikely event. Far from it. Each truly is as each is manifested—self-manifested—in the dual but integral actions of summons and acknowledgment. This is so despite the charming suggestion in the text that Isaiah butts into a question asked of nobody in particular, as though the prophetic vocation were up for grabs and Isaiah makes a bid.

The above side trip into Isaiah is to be charged neither to Scharlemann nor to divine inspiration. It seems to be apposite, nonetheless.

JULIAN N. HARTT

1

The Pathos of
Community in
Contemporary Culture

The Self and the Corporation

SEVERAL THINGS in the general theme of these lectures require
preliminary identification. For this purpose we begin with *theological reflection*. At the present time in this country the phrase is
more likely to denote a performance by a theologian than an
intellectual discipline, almost as though whatever a theologian
happens to be talking about when he is wearing his professional
hat is ipso facto theology. The views of theology of the lecturers
in this series are not that liberal. On the other hand "theological
reflection" is not used here as a device or occasion for lambasting
liberal politicians and humanistic educators for sins against God,
biblical morality, the Christian family, the neighborhood school,
and free enterprise. What theological reflection is to mean more
positively will appear in the course of these lectures.

The second preliminary identification must treat *critique*. A
long time ago Fowler had this to say about the word itself: *"critique
is in less common use than it was, & . . . there is some hope of
its dying out."*[1] Perhaps his other hopes panned out better than
that one. In this country the enormity of the sin has been amplified by making a verb out of *critique: critiquing* goes on all over
the place; along with *dialoguing*. In a somewhat more serious vein
it is to be noted that a critique is more than an ordinary analytical
review. It betokens an effort to get at something fundamental,
something in that sense radical; not necessarily something bad

1

or wrong but, rather, something that needs disclosing or uncovering, and, thereafter, careful evaluation. Thus a critique endeavors to make available something needed for an enlargement and clarification of one's self-understanding and of one's understanding of the world. Hence over the portals of *critique* one ought ideally to descry these words: "You will know the truth, and the truth will make you free."[2]

The most vexatious task in these preliminary identifications is to provide a sketch of *modernity* as free of valuational prejudgments as possible. Modernity unquestionably generates valuational resonances; the rush to judgment is to be avoided.

So modernity is not immediately to be cashed in as "contemporary culture." Much that is contemporary is not really modern; one thinks of people who decry modernity as a spirit in which there is no health or beauty. Moreover, one has no choice in respect to contemporaneity; those who are together on the moving knife-edge of time are contemporaries willy-nilly. But one need not be modern in essential spirit; in respect to that there are choices to be made.

Other valuational resonances of modernity are prompted by announcements that the postmodern age has dawned. Some hear these as gladsome tidings, comparing postmodern to postoperative in the clinical sense: now the patient is sure to get better having been relieved of an acute malignancy. But others are acutely discomfited by news of the arrival of the postmodern age, fearing that many pleasant things, and some very precious, will soon disappear or will persist in strange unpalatable amalgams.

I do not propose here to give much attention to the threat or promise of postmodernity. The overriding concern is first and foremost fairly to delineate modernity. For this purpose a slender clue is found in the derivation of *modern*: it comes from the Latin *modo*, which means "just now," "lately," "presently." Slender help indeed: it promises to make "modern" synonymous with "contemporary." Or, worse, it encourages the swift elevation of "modern" to an honorific: modern, three cheers! Whereupon people who consider themselves thoroughly modern view great masses of humanity as living in historical-cultural backwaters. Not that they huddle there in a lamentably different time zone.

2

Rather, the creative essence of modernity is not yet embodied in their common life.

The presumption of the enlightened in so viewing the masses as locked in historical-cultural backwaters has a useful consequence. It calls attention to modernity as *ethos*. Modernity thus is a defining mentality or spirit expressed in a given society; it is unevenly incarnate there, no doubt, but it imparts to that social order a distinctive character. In a biological-genetic metaphor, that ethos is a set of dominant characteristics.

So modernity can be viewed as set of dominant characteristics not meaningfully attributed either to earlier historical periods or to other societies in any stage of their histories. No doubt some of these features have appeared many times in other cultural constellations. Concentration on that phenomenon lends credibility, for the credulous, to the proverbial wisdom that there is nothing new under the sun. The spirit of modernity sets little store by that hoary adage. For the modern spirit one thing is surely new: a refusal to believe that there is nothing new under the sun.

Other dominant characteristics of modernity are imbued with valuational elements. Prima facie "modern" does not mean better or worse relative to anything earlier or otherwise different. Nevertheless, it is very hard not to think of the present world as more desirable in many if not all respects than any other period in the history of our culture and than any other culture, contemporary or not. Those who do not share these sentiments and convictions are likely to be written off as a romantic and antiquarian. Admiration for T. S. Eliot's poetry does not predictably soften judgment on his regard for the thirteenth century.

Assuming, then, that modernity functions as a spirit permeating the "organs" of a society, though assuredly not every "cell," I venture to identify some of those salient characteristics.

1. *Early and late, modernity betokens a disposition to believe that the imperial errors of the past have been overcome at last and forever.* Many ages have been flattered by savants and prophets who exposed the sins and shortcomings of other peoples and other times. What is singular about this disposition of modernity is the sublime confidence in the once-for-all correction of those capital errors.

THE CRITIQUE OF MODERNITY

The attack of the Enlightenment on superstition is a prime expression of this confidence in the process of history. Consider, for example, the Enlightenment assault on traditional Christianity. Traditional Christianity looks to God for the real and permanent resolution of the human predicament since God is infinitely more powerful and more wise and more righteous altogether than humankind which for its massive corruption deserves everlasting punishment. The classical version of Christianity thus proclaims a destiny for humankind beyond the space-time historical world. That destiny everlastingly divides humankind into the community of the blessed and the aggregation of the damned. So Christianity celebrates a good incomparably superior to any earthly good open to human attainment. Finally, Christianity claims access to truth beyond the farthest and deepest reach of human cognitive capabilities. All its decisively important principles are derived from or constitute the content of revelation.

The modern attack on traditional Christianity, prosecuted with such remarkable energy and brilliance in the eighteenth century, persists into the present. Some philosophers and some theologians are convinced that that war has been won and humankind is the better for that; no doubt the postmodern world will move on to larger and livelier game. Even so, it is a mistake to construe modernity as hostile to all religion or to religiousness as such. Traditional Christianity was an *imperial* error because it produced a world-decisive deflection of human energy and intelligence from a rational and truly humane management of human affairs. In Marx's terms, Christianity systematically confused historical-social evils with metaphysical ones. So Christians believed that having the right attitude toward poverty, pestilence, class dominance, and mass oppression was the acme of wisdom as well as the imperative of proper piety. That right attitude, that ordained passivity, rested on the belief that these evils are God's will. In Freud's terms, Christianity, and perhaps religion as such, is the neurotic projection of real anxieties, guilts, and wishes upon illusory objects.

There is ample reason for this invocation of Marx and Freud. They supply capital expressions of a dominant ingredient of modernity. That is an unyielding resolution to put human well-being and human destiny altogether into human hands—into the *right* human hands. Marx and Freud are, moreover, premier

4

diagnosticians of modern "false consciousness." They discern a distortion of human being so pervasive, inclusive, and powerful that a correct perception of it presupposes a real transcendence of this systemic pathology. A transcendence real first as a novel possibility mysteriously resident in the pathology itself; then real as an actuality endowed with revolutionary potency. But not, of course, a transcendence divinely certified. It is, rather, a level of perception and understanding and a kind of therapeutic strategy attained by scientific rationality.

A second dominant characteristic of modernity has close connections with the first one, close but not transparently logical or rational.

2. *Both nature and history, cosmos and humankind, are subject to a law of irreversible development.* This law is evolution construed in Darwinian terms. That change is a reality-pervading principle, is a metaphysical conviction of great age and perennial power. As this principle persists in modernity, it decrees that change in the natural world is everywhere ordered. In ancient language, flux and logos are the primordial coordinates of the cosmic scheme; what is left to philosophers and thereafter to scientists to do is to figure out how the two principles are related to each other. But perhaps history, understood as the career of humankind through time, is also law-structured; so that persons either naturally perspicacious beyond the reach of normality or divinely inspired are able accurately to predict the future of their world and perhaps the consummating future of humankind altogether. A deep yearning for such an affirmation displays remarkable hardihood. In many cultures, and in Western civilization for a long time, this yearning was exploited most systematically and most effectively by religions. Thus seers and prophets and oracles. Thus also the fascinating history of measures taken in some religions to discredit the "futurists," so to speak, of other religions: the religion of Israel places witchcraft and necromancy under very severe interdiction; members of the early Christian community are warned against false messiahs and unlicensed miracle workers.

In the modern world social philosophers have preempted the role of future-descrying; so far, that is, as intellectually respectable people are concerned. Of these modern prophets none has been so influential as Karl Marx. The fact that his predictions about capitalism have not yet been fulfilled has not greatly diluted the faith of his followers in his discovery of the "iron laws of history." The sturdiness of this faith reminds us that propositions and proclamations about the future cannot be falsified so long as that future is indefinitely postponed. It is written, "Faith is the substance of things hoped for . . . "³ That "substance" is not open to present objective inspection.

Events since the summer of 1914 have violently cured modernity of an earlier identification of progress with the cosmic-historical law of development. They have in fact put a dagger of suspicion against that part of the law stipulating *irreversibility*. Fundamental elements of that cure were present in modernity well before this century of total war and Holocaust. One of these curative elements was the devastating attack on teleology launched in the eighteenth century. That is to say that the modern law of development dispenses with *purpose*. In the life sciences there are linguistic residues of teleology but they are useful fictions, not transcriptions of objectively real processes and relations. Randomness supplants directorial purpose.

Here again Marxian thought is a formidable expression of one of the "hemispheres" of the modern mind. According to that view even the greatest of all humanistic revolutions, indeed the history-consummating one, will come to pass not because its devoted agents *will* it but because it is the necessary operation of the world historical dialectical process.

3. *A third dominant characteristic of modernity is an unresolved ambiguity, conceptual and passional, about continuity and discontinuity.* This ambiguity envelops the understanding of history. It is also present in the understanding of the relation of self to society.

Early in the eighteenth century Vico (1668–1744) called attention to the distinctive reality of human historical existence vis-à-vis the realm of nature. Thus *historicality* emerges as a compelling correction for received doctrines of human nature as a fixed substance only superficially modified by its passage through space, time, and culture. But the notion (before long to become a doctrine and then a dogma of modernity) that human being is sui generis as historical (that is, as characterized essentially by *historicality*) does not of itself speak decisively to the issue of continuity versus discontinuity. So far this is similar to the situation in contemporary Darwinian theories. In both fields there is considerable pressure for a resolution in favor of continuity. This does not mean that the continuity principle is monopolized by philosophical-scientific naturalists with their great rallying cry, "No breaks in the chain of causation!" The penchant for monistic explanatory concepts and systems is a very old affair in human history; it has had many powerful religious expressions. Which is to say that a putatively infrangible causal order can as easily be given an idealistic or spiritualistic reading as any other; Leibniz and Hegel come to mind. It depends on what counts as a cause. Thereafter one needs to know how causal agents, whatever they are, are thought to be connected.

Despite the passion for some kind of uniformitarian causal principle, discontinuity has its partisans in the contest for the mind and heart of modernity. Few of these have had the wit and delayed-action influence of Kierkegaard in espousing the individual's indefeasible reality and value.

The demand for an unbroken causal continuum does not itself legislate what is to count as a cause. So here one expects great differences in construing what constitutes the individual; that is, what his or her core of reality is. And again it is important to see how these presumptively integral and autonomous individuals are thought to be related to one another. The dominant interest in this question is much more existential than scientific or abstractly philosophical. What kind of beings are we? What are we in the process of becoming? Traditional answers to such questions are frequently proposed with more stridency than cogency.

It is a commonplace that a dominant characteristic of modernity is an unresting desire for *autonomy*. In its infancy the modern spirit struggled successfully to throw off the tyrannous yoke of authoritarian institutions such as the church, dynastic monarchical regimes, and birthright aristocracies. Eventually the modern self views autonomy as an indispensable condition for the fulfilling of one's existence as an individual. To be a law unto oneself becomes the essence of realized individuality.

Is, then, the idea of a social continuum a piece of metaphysical fiction, is it a chunk of indigestible dogma left behind by an authoritarian age? Is society really a collection of discontinuous atomistic individuals whose interrelationships are adventitious, fortuitous, and determined by the willful expression of the interests of essentially discrete selves? How is it possible for the *nuclear* family to be constituted by *atomic* selves?

Put in terms so stark, doctrinaire individualism may have few subscribers. One of the main reasons for reluctance to buy the pure doctrine is empirical: how many of such self-defined and self-subsistent individuals does anybody know? That self boasts an attribute traditional theology reserved for God alone: *aseity,* that is, absolute self-completeness and perfect autonomy. Perhaps that God, alienated by the harsh treatment accorded him by modern thinkers, decided to go underground and reappear as the modern autonomous human self. This fanciful suggestion has at least one warrant, Sartre's existentialist self: "To be man means to reach toward being God. Or if you prefer, man fundamentally is the desire to be God."[4]

There is another reason for doubting that there is a golden future for the perfectly autonomous self. I state it as a supposition. Suppose that the modern self were threatened by a *personal* fragmentation that reflected all too faithfully the fragmentation of the *social* world which radical individualism entails? How might that occur?

It would begin innocently enough. The autonomous self ideally is free to do what she or he pleases. But suppose that the pleasings, past present and prospective, are a medley, an aggregate? Suppose, that is, that this self has no command center. So it is incapable of framing and executing a coherent and comprehensive strategy for realizing its aims; thus it is reduced to having to make ad hoc tactical maneuvers in an unending competition for security or power or position or fame—that is, for whatever at a given moment happens to capture its attention and kindle in it a lively interest.

But perhaps this is an unconscionable caricature of the actual situation. True, not many years ago social scientists were speaking seriously about the emergence of just this kind of individual: they called it the Protean Self. Perhaps this ephemeral creature has departed the scene. His erstwhile presence, his brief career, may remind us that modernity contains a kind of discontinuity not yet considered. This is a chasm between what the savants (scientists and philosophers) say about the self and society and what is believed at the grass roots about human being, personal and social. In the academy it is virtually axiomatic that the human self is not only a social being, as ants and bees and some wasps are social creatures. More than that, human beings are internally related to others and to all. Our essential being is *relational*, not *substantival*: there is no indefeasible core of self-being, no private soul. Moreover, we are creatures of the culture in which we are domesticated; we are products of the law-regulated interaction of genetic and environmental factors.

What happens to autonomy on this reading of the human condition? Perhaps the best one can say is, "Autonomy is a relative matter"—not like pregnancy. Or how about this: "What autonomy means, what it actually is, depends on the context"? Thus it makes sense as an ethical-juristic concept: "Your doctor ought to treat you as an *autonomous* person." Autonomy has a function also in psychotherapy: "You don't have to be dominated forever by the image of your father; there is a treatment that will establish your independence from that old lovable/hateful pseudodivinity."

But what about autonomy as an *ontological-theological* principle? The question is hardly put when a theological stopper is applied: "We don't have to answer for character or conduct to a judgmental God since he/she doesn't exist. And even if there were such a God—heaven help us!—it would be very immature on our part, a flat betrayal of autonomy, to cower before it and ask either for forgiveness or for resolution to walk henceforth in his authoritarian and thus not really godly ways."

Beyond the perimeters of the academy, and occasionally within it, autonomy still has an ontological resonance. The doctrine and imagery of the really sovereign individual still commands a large acceptance: a being endowed by nature and nature's God with powers, interests, and rights society is morally bound to respect.

This is the impression that the advocates of free enterprise capitalism wish us to form. One may wonder whether their version of the sovereign self is as widely credited as they seem to believe. In their doctrine the self is the natural profit seeker, the being whose economic interests are fundamental and largely decisive in the ordering of the other interests of the self and of society. The great symbols of this persuasion are profit and private property. Any serious efforts to limit the one and restrict the free use

9

and disposition of the other are represented as political tampering with the natural order. That is just the sort of thing to be expected from idealistic liberals out of touch with the real world.

It is not clear that these doctrines come across as wedded to theoretical egoism. So far as social Darwinism flickers on the horizons of free enterprise thinking we might reasonably suspect that egoism is its philosophical foundation. But we have Professor George Gilder's word for it that the self of free enterprise has an altruistic dimension.[5] And the plethora of philanthropic institutions in this country have long been celebrated as monuments to the potency of benevolence, free and unstinting, in American society.

Granted an optimal assessment of such defenses of free enterprise philosophy, they leave largely untouched the question how this autonomous individual perceives his or her relationships with others. Are these relations fundamentally competitive? Is social life really a scene of conflict? Are other people one's enemies or one's prey? Is their ostensible neutrality a ruse to catch one off guard?

Those latter questions are stained with Sartrian-existentialist colors. Whatever their provenance or coloration, they invite rejection on these shores as too extreme. Happily, the founding fathers of the social philosophy on which a great deal of public policy rests for its justification, utilitarianism, had a more comforting perspective. Hume, for instance, discovered a natural fellow feeling in the repertory of moral sentiments. Adam Smith, though not in the bible of capitalist doctrine, made much of sympathy.

But these theories are cold comfort and pallid assurances for most autonomous selves in this stage of contemporary culture. It is gratifying to learn from whatever source that there are blessed ties that bind us one to another. We appreciate assurances that we are really capable of spontaneous participation in the joys and sorrows of other members of a loving community. So perhaps human beings are not solitary beasts of prey whose alliances with others are dictated not by trust or love but by the harsh necessities of the struggle for existence. But how *real* are these beloved communities? Does their nurturing *really* prepare one for a secure and fulfilling life in the great world whose behavioral laws are at best amoral?

These questions draw ambiguous answers. Out of these ambiguities comes a critique very little influenced by contemporary social-scientific theory. Nor does it display much affinity for the pronouncements and prophecies of the great nay-sayers of modernity, Marx, Nietzsche, and Freud.

Each of these is a master of "the hermeneutics of suspicion," a telling phrase used by Paul Ricoeur in his essay on Freud.[6] Each of these is confident that behind the facade of the modern conventional world the real moving forces in human affairs, the actual determinants of human destiny, are relentlessly at work. Each, thus, is a diagnostician of false consciousness. They do not agree with one another on the nature of these mightly disguised forces. But they do agree that false consciousness is not to be confused with such deceits and exercises in hypocrisy as punctuate, if they do not define, everyday conventionalized consciousness. *That is, we are all victims of false consciousness: it is a social system, it is not a personal venture into moral delinquency.*

I just said, "We are all victims." Not quite all: the diagnostical masters themselves must have been functionally immune from that systemic pathology, "false consciousness." None has the stance revealed in that great prophetic confession in Isaiah: "All we like sheep have gone astray; we have turned every one to his own way" (53:6 RSV). True, Nietzsche's hero, Zarathustra, confesses that he had once been laid low by that deadly disease of the spirit, despair, and had felt the sting of nihilism, that philosophical scorpion. And Freud's letters reveal that his struggle with the Oedipal complex was excruciatingly painful. Nonetheless, Freud and Nietzsche are as confident as Marx that they had seen through the facades of conventionalized existence, social and personal. They believe they have grasped the realities thus disguised. So they were empowered and licensed by apprehended truth to read the future.

"So . . .empowered." Did we overlook, fail to hear, the connection? Perhaps we are back with a medical-clinical metaphor: if one really knows the pathology, one can derive from it the prognosis; the prognosis if treatment is available and the prognosis if none is available. The rightly diagnosed disease will run its course to an appointed end unless . . . ; or, in any case . . . .

Let us leave the clinical metaphor to its own fate. The great "masters of suspicion" do not agree with one another on human destiny; Marx alone of the three predicts a sublime fulfilling of the human possibility. Yet since they are all humanists they say No! to things in culture and the self that have to be overcome, or at least neutralized, for human being to live with self-acceptance and in some kind of affirming community.

The critique of modernity to which we now turn shares one conspicuous feature with these great critics. That is a lively suspicion that what appears to be so massively real that we are condemned to live in its shadow all our years and yield everlasting obeisance to it and confine our hatred of it to indistinct impotent mutterings—a suspicion that this ostensibly omnipotent and ubiquitous social system may prove to be *unreal* as well as immoral.

A consideration of this critique is the second part of the business of this paper. We shall leave to its conclusion any serious consideration of whether such a grass-roots critique has a greater weight in modifying the world than the heavy artillery of professional critics and properly ordained prophets.

The Dialectic of Community and Corporation

The critique of suspicion to which we now turn heavily capitalizes a distinction between *community* and the general society so far as it is dominated by the *corporation*. Community is grounded in kinship and face-to-face relationships. Its beliefs and values are traditional. Whether codified or not, these traditions are accepted as truth and wisdom vouchsafed to the progenitors of the community. It is part of the natural theology of the community to believe that the progenitors were in touch with the divine order.[7] Accordingly, the community understands faith to be a dual reality. The members of a community covenant to live by its traditional rules and precepts. Thus they credit the "faith of our fathers, living still." And they endeavor to relate to one another *faithfully*, that is, in trust and truthfulness and loyalty. Bona fides are certificates of membership in the community.

Covenant is one of the blessed words in the self-understanding of community. As image and concept covenant is a striking element in America's natural theology (= civil religion). It is part of the biblical heritage; it carries in it a faith in divine election (calling). Thus this nation is "the almost chosen people." The

Puritan inspiration was to create the kingdom of God in America.
Here they built the ramparts of a New Jerusalem.

> O beautiful for patriot dream
> That sees beyond the years
> Thine alabaster cities gleam
> Undimmed by human tears!

The Constitution is revered as a solemn covenant drawn up
under divine auspices. It is before God that this nation through
its duly constituted representatives covenants forever to consider,
or make, all men free and equal; and to provide appropriate
redress at law where freedom or equality has been unjustly
restricted or denied.

There is little need to be reminded that a doctrine of divine
providence goes with this natural theology of creation. This nation
has prospered and become the most powerful and richest in all
history because God particularly provides for its well-being. And
he will continue to do so just so long as the successive generations
keep the faith with its covenant vows and their Guarantor. Again
the words of a well-known hymn come to mind:

> Thy love divine hath led us in the past;
> In this free land by Thee our lot is cast;
> Be Thou our Ruler, Guardian, Guide, and Stay,
> Thy Word our law, Thy paths our chosen way.[8]

For so long as we keep the faith . . . Violation of covenant has
persistently been invoked to explain why severe crises in this
country's history have been allowed by that same God to threaten
the very life of his chosen people. The God of Covenant exacts
just requital for those willful violations. I think that the sublimest
expression of this doctrine is the following formidable passage
from Lincoln's Second Inaugural address:

> Fondly do we hope, fervently do we pray, that this mighty scourge
> of war may speedily pass away. Yet, if God wills that it continue
> until all the wealth piled by the bondman's two-hundred and fifty
> years of unrequited toil shall be sunk, and until every drop of blood
> drawn with the lash shall be paid by another drawn with the sword,
> as it was said three thousand years ago, so still it must be said, that
> the judgments of the Lord are true and righteous altogether.

Somewhat less majestic expressions of solemn confidence in
God's retributive justice abound in contemporary conservative

piety. There a precipitous decline in sexual morals and rejection of the traditional home and marriage and a willful failure to acknowledge the diabolical threat of godless Communism have prompted God to diminish America's power abroad and amplify the threat of anarchy at home. Then comes the promissory note: if the people will clean up its sex life and renew its commitment to marriage and the family and go back to church and vote to reestablish military superiority over God's enemies, all will be well.

Biblical notions of providence are thus grievously abused. Despite the abuses covenant remains as an indispensable element of the civil religion, America's natural theology; indispensable and severely conflicted. Hence the question: What makes it so difficult for this element of the "faith of our fathers" to enjoy a tranquil and fertile life at the grass roots of contemporary culture? The question leads into an autobiographical detour.

The town in which I spent my adolescent years is a place virtually immortalized by Hubert Humphrey's celebrations of it: Doland, South Dakota. During those years in Doland we heard over and over again the solemn and for us wholly persuasive proclamation of the national covenant ideal; not just on Memorial Day, either, though that was the high point in the civil liturgical year. Like scores of towns on the plains, Doland was created by the Chicago and Northwestern Railroad. That instrument of divine providence had acquired the land; radicals claimed it was by a swindle. Then the Northwestern sold lots around the station and water tank. And people came and bought the lots and built homes; and a school house was built; and a church; and some stores. The community that thus came to be was named DOLAND, named by the railroad. (The local lore offered two versions of the provenance of that name. One had it that a member of the family of a mogul of the Northwestern was so named. The other version was that he had a horse of that name.)

So one could hardly say that this community came to be by way of covenant. Real estate contracts with the land agents of the railroad were foundational documents for the town, to be sure. It is unlikely that they were called covenants. The word itself was not that common except in relation to the nation. It is unlikely that even the founders of the Methodist Episcopal church in Doland made much of a flourish of conventional language in its institution. The church was built because you couldn't have a *real* town without a church—Americans are God-fearing people, after all. People still say that, from pulpits high and pulpits lowly.

Hubert Humphrey never tired of paying tribute to Doland as a model of authentic community. His devotion is a poignant chapter in America's ritualistic celebration of village life. Nonetheless, one must note that towns were commonly founded for purposes very distantly related to the convenantal tradition; in that respect Doland was not unique. Moreover, the town, frequently and fervently celebrated as *community*, did not always give off the highest ethical resonances. Warmth, generated by a strong sense of belonging; a feeling of obligation to alleviate the suffering of the neighbor, whether or not he or she was kin;[9] readiness to improve the common life: these were important manifestations of "town spirit." (Anybody who had said "ethos" would have been some kind of itinerant show-off.) Trust and trustworthiness were also highly esteemed. A sign over the cash register in the Doland Hardware Store read: "In God we trust; all others pay cash." That was amusing even though religiously questionable: surely Mr. Payne wouldn't have refused credit to *Jesus*! Anyway, that sign didn't square with an important moral fact. One of the supreme accolades to moral character was, "His word is as good as his bond." So trustworthiness was to be taken seriously as part of the Boy Scout code because its value was underscored in community life, in family, school, and business. These are admirable qualities, worthy ideals. But they did not include everything needful for moral education. Consider for example the legendary openness of the prairie town to all comers. But when city folk came to Doland, they had some explaining to do as well as wonders to relate. They were queried thus: How is it possible to live in a place where you don't know the first *real* thing about your neighbors? Is it true your house is locked up day and night? And look at those hordes of people who really aren't Americans: aren't they the chief suppliers of recruits for the "criminal element" in your city?

Behind these predictable provincial queries there was a profound dubiety about the *strangeness* of the city. This uneasiness was easily converted into suspicion and hostility. Thus the question, Isn't *that* kind of society really inimical to sound

15

Christian-American values?[10] There was the suspicion. Thence to hostility focused on social structures and forces embodying that threat: big business, especially Wall Street; machine politics; large bureaucracies of all sorts. All of these manifested an indifference, profound and unyielding, to personal integrity and moral worth. They really did not care about the traditional values and beliefs that had made America great. Their real and sovereign divinity was "the bitch goddess, Success."

There was another and equally powerful suspicion, namely, that the spiritual center of the nation was shifting implacably to the city along with more and more of the population. Did not this mean that strange ways accompanied and reinforced by strange divinities—alien ways and alien gods—would dominate the future?

So a critique of modernity emerged, a critique in what is now the received sense: a largely negative assessment of the shape, momentum, and direction of contemporary culture.

The heart of this critique of suspicion is to be found in the conviction that *community* and *corporation* are locked in deadly conflict for possession of the heart and soul of the nation. The fear that the engagement is going against community is part of what is intended by "the pathos of community."

Covenant

Corporation is used here to denote impersonal social structures replete with great power and devoid of soul. A corporation governs with a view to advancing its own interests. One of its dominant interests is aggrandizing its power without displaying excessive tenderness for moral scruples not clearly and firmly embodied in legal statutes.

But now a cautionary note. Our interest in the conflict between community and corporation does not yet run toward an evaluation of the moral case for either. It lies in probing for the moral core of the conflict. That is, what defines the essential difference between community and corporation, as the difference is conceived and treasured in this critique of modernity? I suggest that it is the conflict between *covenant* and *contract*.

As this conflict is seen from the perspective of community, covenant is the moral heart of community and contract is the

16

amoral heart of the corporation. True, both covenant and contract are promissory. But the corporation's interest is self-serving and submoral despite all the flourishes in juristic rhetoric of "fairness," "equity," and the like.

The moral heart of community is covenant. The moral foundation of covenant is promise, or pledge, a gesture of self-binding involvement, an engagement of the deep and (so far) real self. In covenant, persons bind themselves one to another "for better and for worse." They bind themselves in freedom; and this in such wise that some aspect or degree of freedom is freely given over. So far, then, covenantal promise is unconditional. It is not, "I will be faithful until such time as something more interesting or more profitable materializes." Covenantal promise is, rather, "So long as we live we will be to another thus and not otherwise."

I have designedly used here the language of traditional Christian marriage covenants in which fidelity is clearly linked with perpetuity. The biblical provenance of this union is unmistakable. And that has a bearing on conservative Christian criticism of contemporary culture. In that critique a cardinal element in the general slackening of the moral fiber of the nation is a readiness to nullify the most basic and solemn promises the moment they complicate the pursuit of self-gratification.

Unconditionality of promise in this sense, or perhaps in any other, is a contestable matter, no doubt, though in fact it is not contested in America's natural theology of community. Another feature of the covenant community is also accepted in that outlook as beyond peradventure of doubt. That is the fact that the covenant community is *there* before the individual's pledge of self to it. And it will faithfully receive one's death. The metaphor of family comes to mind. One is born into it, it does not exist in response to a command of one's will; one can will to leave it but one cannot will to join it. This holds for the nation conceived as a community of covenant. One may join it by "naturalization," that is, by acquiring a new "nature." In more general terms, membership in a covenant community is understood as a gift. Behind the gift, expressed in the gift, is love. Hence to be treated as a member of a community is to be a recipient of affirming love. And if one cannot lay claim to that, then all the other rights and privileges of membership are deeply compromised. This is to say that the affectional foundation of covenant community is love, other-regarding and other-cherishing love.

The biblical inspiration of this conviction is nowhere expressed more poignantly than by the prophet Hosea.

> When Israel was a child, I loved him, and out of Egypt I called my son. The more I called them, the more they went from me; they kept sacrificing to the Baals, and burning incense to idols. Yet it was I who taught Ephraim to walk, I took them up in my arms; but they did not know that I healed them. I led them with cords of compassion, with the bands of love, and I became to them as one who eases the yoke on their jaws, and I bent down to them and fed them. (11:1–4, RSV)

The progress of the heart from ego-centered and ego-gratifying love to love of others for and as themselves has long been viewed as the essence of the moral education a community ought to provide; and not simply through the offices of religion. Part of that education is learning to respect the rights of others, or suffer the consequences; suffering the consequences is part of that learning experience.

Another element of the faith of the covenant community is its *historicity*. As we have seen this includes the events in which the community originated. There we noted the contrast between the known origins of the western town and the mythologized origin of the nation. Was the Chicago and Northwestern Railroad an instrument of that providence which shaped the creation of the nation? The question is an odd one. The persistent assimilation of biblical providence to the history of this nation has often produced oddities. Be that as it may, God's guiding hand is seen in the provision of the great leader sent to save the people when they are threatened with extinction either by the brute power of external foes or by the lure of heathenish religious practices at home. So God sends Elijah to save Israel from Jezebel's heathenish seductions; then he sends "ravens"[11] to feed his prophet when Elijah had to hide in a remote wilderness to escape Jezebel's lethal fury.[12]

The historicity of the community comes to light in the story it tells not only about its origin but about its destiny. The great past and the ultimate future are brought together. The life of the community and of its faithful members is thus defined by that alpha and omega. The end is fully and truly implicated in the beginning.

Accordingly *destiny* is the imperial image-concept with which the covenant community appropriates the future. Absolute assurance is the personal cognitive correlate of destiny. The assurance is absolute because God is its cause. The great tomorrow is assured not because the community is so powerful or its members so saintly but because God is faithful altogether. Beyond all the vicissitudes of historical existence a realm of everlasting peace and perfect happiness awaits the faithful community. Accordingly the perfect freedom in which God created the covenant community and determines the blessed outcome of its history is reflected in the freedom of the faithful. They are delivered from bondage to fateful worldly powers, so here and now they enjoy freedom from anxiety about the ultimate outcome of life and history.

This understanding of destiny as the absolutely assured future of the covenant community seems very far removed from modern pieties dealing with human freedom in relation to destiny. Liberal Protestant theology was disposed to make human freedom a reality, a metaphysical given, so fundamental that God must acknowledge it and relate to it as to an objective limitation upon his own freedom. In this way freedom as the necessary condition for the creation and enhancement of the human good is acknowledged and diligently pursued by all right-thinking persons and, of course, by God. Given this feature of liberal theology, there was little doubt that the emergence of an enduring ethical community, like Kant's Realm of Ends, was in the cosmic-historical-divine works.

But there is another and very different doctrine concerning the relation of community and destiny. Professor John Plamenatz had this to say about the Marx-Engels position:

> Now it may well be that Marx and Engels thought of the future communist society as a community of friends and neighbors. But they also thought of it as an industrial society more advanced technologically than the capitalist economy of their day. It was to combine the advantages of material progress with the close human ties which this progress, in its capitalist phase, had so largely destroyed.

It was to restore these ties at a higher level, a level consistent with aspirations to freedom and self-realization unknown to pre-capitalist societies. But how it was to do this neither Marx nor Engels explained. The attempt to explain it would no doubt have seemed to them Utopian dreaming. In their philosophy, though to predict is reasonable, to explain how what you predict might be accomplished, how society and production should be organized to achieve it, is unreasonable. A convenient philosophy which allows you to make large promises without making it clear just what you are promising![13]

The secular piety of the everyday realm of contemporary culture manifests a remarkably similar ambiguity about the ideal relationship of community with the large impersonal social structures necessary for the management of a complex macrocivilization. This ambiguity is a response to the ascent of the corporation to dominance not only as the sovereign social structure but also as the imperial image of the rational organization of human resources. The corporation has emerged as the now and future lord of human creation.

Corporation

For our purposes *corporation* denotes more than its economic formations. Wherever social organization is designed, preserved, and corrected to function as a mechanism, that is, a thing of reciprocating parts in the utilization of energy, there is the corporation. In the modern world it has become an entity endowed with special attributes of rationality, efficiency, and utility. Other features are closely related to these: a special value given to technique; impersonality combined with pseudoindividuality.

The surrogate for morality at (as) the heart of the corporation is *contract*. The corporation is a mutual benefit association or at least reciprocating benefit based on quid pro quo: something for something, according to agreements in which the interests of the contracting parties are set forth and provisions stipulated for the satisfactions of said interests in case of default or breach by either of the contracting parties.

On its face contract greatly resembles covenantal *promise*, suggesting that contract is a jurisprudential-economic descendent of promise. This inference is misleading. Justice Oliver Wendell Holmes made it clear that contract leaves promise, morally understood, far behind.[14] For contract necessarily assumes quid pro quo: something materially specifiable to be gained from the agreement. And while it is true that the promise (the second party of a covenant) stands to gain from the relationship thus created or acknowledged, the quid he or she offers may derive from the promise and not be a condition of its validity. The important difference, however, rests on the ambiguity of *enrichment* or gain. The highest level of covenantal promise is the pledge of mutuality in and of love. From this each and all derive enrichment of being. It does not follow that gain or benefit is the controlling objective for either or any parties, so far as that is subjected to calculative reason. On the other hand, corporation contract is unavoidably literal in understanding enrichment or profit. A material improvement for both parties is the controlling objective; and it is, or ought to be, a product of calculative reason.

Another kind of historical consideration concerns a significant change in the moral climate of this country in understanding contract. I cite at some length a striking passage from an article by Professor Friedrich Kessler.

> The individualism of our rules of contract law, of which freedom of contract is the most powerful symbol, is closely tied up with the ethics of free enterprise capitalism and the ideals of justice of a mobile society of small enterprisers, individual merchants and independent craftsmen. This society believed that individual and cooperative action left unrestrained in family, church and market would not lessen the freedom and dignity of man but would secure the highest possible social justice. It was firmly convinced of a natural law according to which the individual serving his own interest was also serving the interest of the community. Profits can be earned only by supplying consumable commodities. Freedom of competition will prevent profits from rising unduly. The play of the market if left to itself must therefore maximize net satisfactions. Justice within this framework has a very definite meaning. It means freedom of property and of contract, of profit making and of trade . . . . Freedom of contract thus receives its moral justification. The "pre-stabilized harmony" of a social system based on freedom of enterprise and perfect competition sees to it that the "private autonomy" of contracting parties will be kept within bounds and will work out to the benefit of the whole.

THE CRITIQUE OF MODERNITY

With the decline of the free enterprise systems due to the innate trend of competitive capitalism towards monopoly, the meaning of contract has changed radically. Society, when granting freedom of contract, does not guarantee that all members of the community will be able to make use of it to the same extent. On the contrary, the law, by protecting the unequal distribution of property, does nothing to prevent freedom of contract from becoming a one-sided privilege. Society, by proclaiming freedom of contract, guarantees that it will not interfere with the exercise of power by contract. Freedom of contract enables enterprisers to legislate by contract and, what is even more important, to legislate in a substantially authoritarian manner without using the appearance of authoritarian forms. Standard contracts in particular could thus become effective instruments in the hands of powerful industrial and commercial over-lords enabling them to impose a new feudal order of their own making upon a vast host of vassals . . . . This spectacle is all the more fascinating since not more than a hundred years ago contract ideology had been successfully used to break down the last vestiges of a patriarchal and benevolent feudal order in the field of master and servant."[15]

Thus the principles of freedom and justice are reworked to suit the interests of the corporation.

We turn now to other features of the corporation deemed to be hostile to community and therefore antithetical to an authentic humanism.

1. *Rationality.* The corporation's understanding of rationality transvaluates or revolutionizes traditional views of the life of reason in human affairs. Some of the important particulars of this large claim are the following.

First, the corporation gives all but unrivaled priority to the technical employment of rationality, hitherto simply identified as technical reason. For our purposes the prime expressions of this are the weight given to calculative functions and to the mastery of technique.

Cost accounting and cost-benefit analysis are not novelties in human organizations. Their application to every area of public policy is a modern development, that is, as the decisive rational method for adjudicating conflicts among various interests. In narrow economic terms the calculation of benefit from the expenditure or use of resources is, of course, profit. The application of the corporation model of cost-benefit calculation seems to require a larger conception of benefit than profit. Larger, perhaps; but surely not divorced from quantification rules. The dream of utilitarians has been largely realized in what are now standard justifications for public policy decisions: the greatest good for the greatest number. That great instrument of calculative technique, the computer, has helped enormously at this point. The figures can be laid out so quickly and in such massive ramifications that one can just *see* there is only one way to go.

Second, the corporation's understanding of rationality gives high priority to the *mastery of technique*. In common usage, *technique* denotes a carefully patterned or stylized craft or skill. The corporation's heavy investment in technique looks to the reproduction to infinity of that patterned skill without respect to personal differences among the people who have acquired it. In more general terms, to master a technique in an important process is an important device for getting ahead in the corporation itself and in the culture which has assimilated the corporation's ethos. This less technical understanding of technique is expressed in the large audiences for training in how to win friends and influence people, how to have your way in conflict situations, and how to have an incredible sex life, etc., etc.

Technique, so understood, encourages the development of a repertory of manipulative strategies. Their employment may yield benign effects, a result more flattering to providence than to moral scruple or altruistic intentions.

2. *Efficiency.* Efficiency is an ideal closely related to the corporation's understanding of rationality. To rationalize an organization is to eliminate wasted motion. To rationalize a machine is to reduce systematically (that is, not randomly or piecemeal) the friction factor, as part of an effort to bring the use of energy and the product into a stable and profitable equation. Looking beyond these narrow denotations of rationalization to larger social application, we might find suggestive this item from a contemporary dictionary: in mathematics, to rationalize is "to eliminate a radical from an equation" (*Random House Dictionary*).

Efficiency calls for maximum emphasis on the usefulness of all the elements of the corporation. The effects of the large social assimilation of this corporation ideal hardly need extensive documentation. Personal relationships as well as corporation welfare are appraised for their usefulness. Friends are people near at hand who have been or might be lured into proving useful for the advancement of one's own interests. Mature friendships are mutual benefit associations of durable utility. Really close dealings, face-to-face relationships, are valuable so far as they allow one of the parties to see himself, his own image, in the eyes of the other; reflecting sunglasses are ideal for this purpose.

3. *Impersonality*. Here we approach the heart of the grass-roots critique of contemporary culture. Here is the charge that the corporation is soulless. The corporation has a brain, that is, a mechanism, a profit-calculating computerlike mind. But it has no heart; its humane benevolent gestures are calculated, practiced, and tax deductible.

The predictable focus of this indictment is *bureaucracy*. A disposition to concentrate on political bureaucracy marks the success of philosophical (= ideological) indoctrination. The doctrine is that big government is inherently evil because it is incurably addicted to meddling with other institutions, such as the market, the family, and the schools. And it is dedicated to running the world through faceless, self-serving, self-perpetuating structures.

Proclamations of this doctrine have scored substantial victories in contemporary politics. But monolithic corporations other than big government have also received a portion of unflattering attention. So you think that IRS has gored you? How about your experience with that GM warranty? How about that new GE toaster that behaved like a missile launcher? And how long did it take you to get that mistake on your MasterCard corrected? And did you ever find out why that Holiday Inn refused to honor your Citicorp Visa? Etc., etc. These are more than complaints about corporate inefficiency. They say that no one up there is paying attention to us; we are getting nothing but recorded messages and printouts harder than a road map to fold or follow.

When these complaints are orchestrated for a cooler critique of contemporary culture, this is what we have; today society is afflicted with *giantism*. Big is good; bigger is better; biggest is best. Strength is good; superiority is better; omnipotence is best. Free enterprise theologians eulogize (eulogize is right: part of a funeral ceremony) competition. On the other hand we are summoned to mourn the dreadful—grisly—dismemberment of AT&T. What does it matter that this company tried to stifle competition? By God, sir, she was *efficient*! In fact AT&T was just one case among many where competition has been engulfed in a *gigantomachy*, the mortal struggle of giants to control the economy in a vital sector and thus dictate to the general society what it shall pay for those goods and services. Even so, one is urged to believe that *bigness as such* is not the problem. The problem is the concomitant loss of the personal dimension. The problem is the creation of impersonal structures to stand between the policymakers and policy administrators on the side of corporation over against the public they are supposed to serve. The diffusion and masking of responsibility within bureaucracies are such that tracking down accountability for decisions appears to be impossible. Bureaucrats can exculpate themselves with, "I was just carrying out orders," or "*I* don't make the policies— *privately* I think they are very poor ones." Etc. When things get so far out of hand that an outraged public demands that *some* culprit be hanged, so to speak, the system provides a scapegoat. If the scapegoat was not very efficient anyway or was afflicted with other character defects, the results of the punitive foray against the inequities of the bureaucracy are deemed acceptable. A few die-hard critics will claim that the clean up was a callous charade allowing the great culprits to go their smiling unredeemed way. In an election year these attacks are written off as "politically motivated." In normal terms they are construed as bitter mouthings of congenital soreheads.

The charge of impersonality has another element. The corporation systematically substitutes the appearance of morality for its reality: the plausible appearance, the persuasive image, is all that really matters. The good for which the corporation lives is its own power. When it is necessary, that is clearly and indispensably useful, a facade of morality is erected and adorned. For the time being, Number One at GM is not going to say, "We really don't care about the safety of our cars." He may very well say, "It is not economically feasible to do such-and-such now, if ever." He will not admit that the lives of thousands may be jeopardized by that policy. It would be grossly unfair to say that he doesn't care about that. The enforceable demands upon his caring derive from his position in the corporation. Anyway, the evidence may not be absolutely conclusive; and there are so many other factors. In any case the corporation exists to make a profit. It makes a profit by making a product that meets a need. But is it a *real* need? There's an abstract philosophical question. People *believe* they need a new car, GM needs a profit. Ancillary to that need is the need of the corporation to convince the public that GM cars are the answer to their prayers. When GM prays now, it does what a lot of smart consumers have been doing for some time: it faces the Far East: the land of the Rising Toyota.

4. *Pseudoindividuality.* A familiar indictment of the corporation is that it systematically practices deception. Now we come to a charge that has a curious metaphysical ring to it. *The corporation in itself is an illusion.* What does this mean? First of all in the eyes of the law the corporation is an "individual." It is written that a corporation is

> in law, [an] organization enjoying legal personality for the purpose of carrying on certain activities. . . . As a legal person, the corporation continues in existence when the organizers lose their connection with it. . . . Legal personality gives the corporation many of the capacities of a natural person; e.g., it can hold property and can even commit crimes. . . . The modern concept of corporate power is that the rights of the participants as well as the conduct of the enterprise must be the subject of managerial discretion.[16]

So the corporation has a *factitious* reality. Not *fictive:* it is not a figment of the imagination, it is not a phantasm. The corporation can do fantastic things, nightmarish; but it is not the stuff of dreams.

Factitious, then. The corporation is an artificial entity, not a natural one. Once in existence, its powers are real enough, in all conscience. As noted, it has "many of the capacities of a natural person" and "can even commit crimes." It can; it does. But does the corporation have an equally natural capacity for being *morally* guilty, not just legally at fault?

In connection with this question we note a powerful disposition in public servants to admit, when the facts are in, having made *mistakes*, mistakes in perception, mistakes in managerial judgment. This is much easier than admitting *moral* culpability. Mr. Nixon admitted that he had made mistakes, not that what he did was morally wrong. Other public figures admit that it is a *mistake* to lie and betray trust, once the facts are out. But they are singularly reluctant to admit to *moral* malfeasance. Perhaps they believe that merely moral malfeasances are not incapacitating for public service.

The second element in the charge of pseudoindividuality is that the corporation systematically treats its subjects as though *they* were pseudopersons. In the medical corporation we are *cases*, actual or potential. In the religious corporation we are souls to be saved or damned; in the meantime to be mulcted. In the economic corporation we are so many ergs in the energy reservoirs and consumers with their brains in the guts—or lower.

Suppose now that such indictments could be sustained. One would then be obliged to ask whether the corporation as such can afford or is able to perceive and treat its people as integral persons and as irreducible moral agents, who therefore are or can be in vivifying and enriching touch with the really real world. It is bad enough to exist as a number coded into the mechanical brain of the corporation with only a problematical reality outside it. It would be modestly gratifying to be treated as a *whole* number; then one could dream of being a prime number, however small. But to be treated as fractions and as rational fractions to boot: that is the curse of pseudopersonality at the individual level.

One of the remarkable and far-reaching achievements of modern theology was the depersonalizing of macro-scale evil. Satan was forced from his horrid throne and stripped of every vestige of individuality. This was the victory of the *demonic* over the *diabolical*. The demonic was retained to signify vast destruction of life and civilization wrought unintentionally. Demonic pertains to the scale of social-cultured effects, not to evil motives of individuals.

The application of this revisionist theological principle to terrible historical events is all too familiar. For example, no one willed the awful suffering caused by World War I. One of the pearls of conventional historical wisdom is the belief that no one intended or prepared for that war. Once under way it developed a demonic logic of its own that had to be followed to the end. But no individual and no committee invented that logic; diabolical malice was not its inspiration. The Marxists claimed that the evil was inherent in the capitalist system itself. The orthodox communists wanted no part of that war: it was the internecine death struggle of rival empires. Let them all go under!

Marx himself exploited this principle of depersonalized macroscale evil in his critique of modernity. In his view the appalling suffering caused by the capitalist domination of the Industrial Revolution was not *willed* by the ruling class. Marx had no reason in principle to deny that some members of that class might be very decent individuals, given the validity of conventional morals. Neither does adherence to St. Augustine's doctrine of Original Sin give one reason in principle to doubt that now and then human beings do good things. For Marx the social system relentlessly and unconsciously (as it were) corrupts conscience. For St. Augustine the human substance as such was bent away from its proper good by a historical act.

Some such distinction between a supervenient reality and personal choices figures in the explanation of why the corporation cannot afford to treat its subjects as integral persons and irreducible moral agents. The corporation does not intend ill for them. But it will not, it cannot, admit that it is fundamentally wrong in its perceptions of its people and in its convictions about their reality and about its own imperial reality. Indeed for the corporation to confess that its perceptions and doctrines were seriously defective might well strike its subjects as a calamity. *So terrific a mea culpa from the corporation would be to abandon the modern self.* This creature has enough troubles without a disaster of that magnitude. The quest for personal identity is already sufficiently harrowing.

The conflicted passion for the discovery of personal identity speaks volumes about the pathos of community and the plight of the self in contemporary culture. Grant Plato's claim that the state is but the self writ large, and the deep and dire suspicions aimed at the corporation receive some illumination. "The corporation has no soul" strongly suggests that the putatively integral and autonomous individual does not have a very firm and dry grip on her or his own soul.

The soul that matters in this connection is not the metaphysical entity so heavily battered by modern winds of scientific-philosophic doctrine. Many Christian theologians have deserted that ship, partly because it seemed important to notify the philosophers that Cartesian mind-body dualism was as unacceptable in the courts of divinity as anywhere else. So that old metaphysical-theological soul is somewhere in limbo. The soul of persistent concern in contemporary culture is a metaphor for a wholehearted (single-willed) commitment to things presumed to dignify personal existence and potentialize its highest aspirations and withal make it a fit member of an ethical community. Given the ascendency of the corporation in contemporary culture, soul in this sense is deeply infected with unreality. Those fair and noble concerns are all decorative, none is substantial. This modern soul is incapable of doing or being anything that makes a palpable difference in the real world. The shape and movement of the real world are determined by drives human beings have in common with other species in the real of nature, those creatures traditionally labeled "lower."

Let it be said again that we are not dealing here with metaphysics. Marx and Engels did not believe they were making metaphysical claims when they assigned decisive causal efficacy to material forces and relationships in accounting for the behavior of societies and of their constituent individuals. So here what do people have in mind when in the normalities of everyday discourse they talk about "the real world"? Idealistic young people are told that the real world is not governed by ethical principles, a fact concealed from them by most of their college teachers. Politicians tell their constituents that the real world lends scant and uncertain encouragement to the pursuit of peace and justice.

What is this real world that appears so persistently in the normalities of everyday discourse? In the mind of the corporation the real world is the arena in which people compete for the advantages of power and place, each for oneself. In this contest quarter is given only when it promises advantage to the winner; it is asked in order to return to the fray down the line; compassion is reserved for the next of kin. In this real world the value of the individual is defined as his productivity as a worker; by the sweat of his brow he not only earns his bread—he earns his reality as well. Hence to be out of work is to be diminished in being. And *retired* means uselessness: exiled from meaningful existence.

Obviously, this picture of the real world of the corporation is incomplete; it might even be a diabolical distortion. It leaves out such estimable things as corporation in the pursuit of the public good, deeds of kindness and heroic endeavors to correct destructive features of the social system, and other ventures inspired by the principle of altruistic love.

The cultivation of these moral adornments of character does not necessarily conflict with the self's drive for power, affluence, and status. Moreover it is probably true that most people prefer to be loved rather than hated, whether or not they would prefer to be hated rather than ignored. But what if being loved prevented one from amounting to something and being somebody in the real world? There is a conservative sentiment to the effect that such a conflict is not a necessary fate lying in wait for the self of free enterprise; perhaps beneficence, altruistic love of others, perhaps of all others, is the triumphantly *real* motive in seeking to maximize profits. Perhaps, too, in a free market the hardy entrepreneurial self really learns to esteem moral substance over moral appearance.

So the mind of the corporation seeks to display sensitivity to moral concerns. As a supervenient individual the corporation may not have a conscience, but its people are free to cultivate one on their own. And so also for other noneconomic interests they may have. Let them believe that man does not live by bread alone, or even by cake. Perhaps in some world that might even be true.

This world, other worlds; the real world, possible worlds. Modernity has given traditional supernaturalism many an enthusiastic thumping; the notion of a plurality of worlds—perhaps an infinity!—is dear to the heart of modernity. Moreover it is a commonplace that every advanced civilization comprises plural realms: science, religion, art, philosophy, common sense, each with its unique claims to importance. Contemporary culture is deeply conflicted on the rank-order of competing realms of value. Thus the inevitable question: which realm "clues" one on the *real* world? From this another question follows: Is the corporation disposed to admit that its answer to that first question is both grossly and subtly defective? Or will it persist in claiming that its tutoring of the self is the bottom line for the moralization of the self, the real world being what it is?

Yet another question obtrudes: Is the self-subject of the corporation an essentially *social* being? Or is it still an atomistic one, self-defining and self-centered, and thus self-referential and self-preferential in all its acts and dispositions? Can that self recognize in sociality an ontological fact? Or is this creature of the corporation constrained to endow sociality with psychological value only, thus something worthy of cultivation for ego purposes? These are questions circling about an institution: a self derivatively social is an image condemned to live in the kingdom of images; the substance and the power of moral reality eludes them all, but not quite altogether.

A theological generation but lately gone from the contemporary scene made a great deal of the threat of meaninglessness. The threat remains. It is expressed in the pathos of community. The flight of the middle class from the city was motivated in part by the threat of meaninglessness. There were more pungent dangers. But there was a powerful feeling that the city is the dominion of the corporation. So one owes it to oneself and to one's family, if any, to find a more human-humane environment where one can *really* live. Thus the quest for community, not just a place but a situation in which one can relate to neighbors as though they were one's brothers and sisters, and be known by them in trust and loyalty and the kindred affections of freedom. The kingdom of the corporation is a rat race. Community is made up of honest-to-God persons, whatever their religious persuasions.

In this pilgrimage there is a strong suggestion of a yearning for the recovery of lost innocence. But is it really possible to make such a retrieval, assuming that innocence is back there or down there to be recovered? Is it given to human beings to turn back the clock, to peel off the psychological and cultural accretions—that second nature indispensable for social coherence and stability—and discover anew a primordial goodness of being?

I am not sure that the quest for self-meaning in an affirming community is clearly animated by such a yearning. But perhaps in it there is a silent and largely disguised hope that the recent past might somehow be nullified in favor of a remoter and dearer past. Not a metaphysical miracle, not a divine efficacious tinkering with time. But a regaining of values and beliefs and attitudes certifiably geared into the really real world. For this purpose, then, a restructuring of the primary institutions of the general society.

Hope of this magnitude runs far beyond achieving damage control. It is the dream of a conservative revolution that would put right and straight everything that is wrong and bent in contemporary culture. Thus the quest for community and the hope for the recovery of lost innocence become politically programmatic.

The program lacks universal appeal; it beggars the dream and coarsens the hope. For the larger part, larger by far, people are seeking an asylum, not a comprehensive revolution. They want a community animated by natural affections, passions and sentiments, "natural" in a pre-Darwinian sense. They seek a community, a homeland in which one can get a fresh grip on lovable goodness and amplify it. Hence a community in which one's value is not assayed for corporation productivity but is esteemed as a unique prime good: an end in itself. Thus a yearning for a wholeness of being: let each be an integer, none a fraction. Let all be constituents, none parts. Let all be members one of another, no longer statistical-mechanical units. Let *personae* go. We want to be, we need to be *persons*.

This yearning (want, need, desire) is much more than a vehement reaction against the hegemony of the corporation. Nor is it merely a product of centuries of Jewish and Christian instruction. It is a metaphysical fact. We ought to suspect religious persuasions that deny or obscure it.

Finally, I believe that the world ahead on the timeline will not be the captive of the corporation. That anxiety is unrealistic. But unrealistic also is any hope for an amplification of community to include the whole human order both near at hand and to the ends of the earth. Some religions *promise so splendid* attainment of communal existence; the wise among them commit it to another world and time. The hope of a humane—not a perfect—social order in the world here below demands the preservation of an unrelenting tension between community and corporation. The corporation cannot live without the contract. Full humanity cannot come to be without the covenant.

Notes

[1]H. W. Fowler, *A Dictionary of Modern English Usage* (New York: Oxford Univ. Press, 1944), p. 99.

[2]John 8:32, Revised Standard Version (RSV).

[3]Hebrews 11:1, Authorized Version.

[4]Jean-Paul Sartre, *Being and Nothingness*, trans. by Hazel E. Barnes (New York: Philosophical Library, 1956), p. 566. He adds: "My freedom is a choice of being God and all my acts, all my projects translate this choice and reflect it in a thousand and one ways" (p. 599).

[5]"The 'essence' of productive work under capitalism is that it is altruistic" (George Gilder, *Wealth and Poverty* [New York: Basic Books, 1981], p. 168.

[6]Paul Ricoeur, *Freud and Philosophy* (New Haven: Yale Univ. Press, 1970), pp. 32–36.

[7]"In many and various ways God spoke of old to our fathers by the prophets" (Hebrews 1:1 [RSV]).

[8]*The Methodist Hymnal* (Nashville: Methodist Book Concern, 1935), p. 496.

[9]In the western town kinship ties were the exception, not the rule.

[10]Nowdays all but universally called "Judeo-Christian." Such are the sterling achievements of ecumenicity.

[11]"Angels," 1 Kings 19 (RSV).

[12]An imposing illustration of a culturally transmuted providence is part of the theology of free enterprise: the doctrine of the Invisible Hand. Let each person do his calculated utmost to improve his position in the market and leave to providence a presumptively efficacious care of the public good. In this way God uses private greed to serve the great social ends of stability and progress. The God thus employed hardly had a respectable alternative. The deists had put him under moral and metaphysical obligation not to tinker with the flawless order he had created.

[13]John Plamenatz, *Karl Marx's Philosophy of Man* (Oxford: Clarendon Press, 1975), p. 296.

[14]Oliver Wendell Holmes, *The Common Law* (Birmingham, Ala.: Legal Classics Library, 1982), pp. 247, 253, 300. I wish to thank Professor Calvin Woodard of the School of Law, University of Virginia, for calling my attention to Holmes's discussion of this issue.

[15]Friedrich Kessler, "Contracts of Adhesion—Some Thoughts about Freedom of Contract," *Columbia Law Review* 63 (1943): 640–41.

[16]*The Columbia Encyclopedia* (New York: Columbia Univ. Press, 1963), p. 493.

RAY L. HART

2

The Dialectic of
Home and Homelessness
Religion, Nature,
and Home

FOREWORDS

IN THE LECTURES that formed the original base of this volume, the authors were charged to identify and characterize certain features of modernity, and to enter upon such critique of them as would warrantably unfold. The problematic upon which my attention centers is that of home and homelessness in the modern world. No motif recurs more often and more plaintively from the beginning of modernity than this: man is homesick and sick of the home he has. Just one year after Galileo published his little pamphlet that was read avidly as far as away as Peking, in which he began the shift of the cosmic center from the earth to the sun, just as quickly John Donne perceived in his poem "An Anatomie of the World" the end of the world as home.[1]

'Tis all in peeces, all cohaerance gone;
All just supply, and all Relation:

The "cohaerance gone" was the sense of natural status and natural relatedness. Now come the haunting words

For every man alone thinkes he hath got
To be a Phoenix, and that then can bee

35

None of that kinde, of which he is, but hee.
Man alone, away from home, a grounded bird, aspiring to be a
phoenix, homesick for the cosmic nest.

To attend to the great humanistic voices and texts of the last
four centuries would be to find a like pathos of homelessness.
There would be occasional protests in epic proportions: William
Blake's poetic rage against "Newton's sleep" and man's death
because he is no longer sourced by nature's vitality, Goethe's
scientific rage against Newton's theory of color that could not
source a painter's vision. The line of pathos is essentially unbroken into so recent a voice as that of Martin Buber. Now not only
is the Jew in diaspora; a universal diaspora has settled over
mankind.

While it is no part of my self-appointed task to sweep the
theme of home and homelessness through the modern period, I
cannot forebear mention of one of the towering figures in its
story, and that as much for what he neglects as for what he
includes. One of the great texts of modernity in respect of home
is Nietzsche's *Thus Spake Zarathustra*. Like Goethe's ancient Faust,
Nietzsche foresaw the fruition of technology, a fruition that would
hand over the earth to human hegemony. For this task, no man,
not even Zarathustra, is ready. Nietzsche's book is addressed to
"Everyone and No One." The "no one" is the one who is at
home in man-up-to-now, the "hearth squatter," the "musty mys-
tifier," "you modern men: you are a conflict and a cross between
plant and ghost."[2] "Everyone" embraces all those, and they are
few, who recognize homelessness on the basis of negative witness,
by the sheer absence of home. The crucial question is whether
the home we are away from, that is absent, is back there (in the
past) and forgotten, or ahead and unenvisaged: modern man is
strung over the abyss between, and awaits the "overture," the
guidance of the "overman." In Part 3 of the book Nietzsche
comes clean: Zarathrustra, the man who has broken with man-
up-to-now, is spoken of as the Convalescent. To convalesce, from
the Greek, means to return (or re-turn toward) home. That return is a willed thrust ahead that is met by something coming
back (a return).[3] Only a man coming back from the future can
give us a past voided of the detritus of man-up-to-now. The
name Zarathustra gives to the coming, returning home, is "the
eternal recurrence of the same." Only in the coincidence of

"Formerly," "Today," and "Tomorrow" through the eternal recurrence of the same can man overcome his revenge against time and the transient.

But Zarathustra had said that modern man's homelessness owed to *two* things, to two revenges: his *ressentiment* against time and transience, *and* his *ressentiment* against the earth. Man-up-to-now is a despiser not only of "it was" and "it might have been otherwise," but a despiser also of the earth and the body. If the eternal recurrence of the same gives man an eternal home in the coincidence of the modes of time, what home offers refuge from the revenge against earth? Without such a home, technology would only give man an instrument for, and equal to, his revenge against the earth. It is an irony worthy of Nietzsche's love of irony that Zarathustra is unable to think the eternal recurrence of the same out of his own resources but must receive it recurrently as an announcement of his animals, the voices of the earth. Yet the earth as the home of nonvengeful man remains Nietzsche's unthought thought.

I have taken this detour through Nietzsche in order to point up the proclivity of modern thinkers for treating home and homelessness in relation to time and history to the neglect of earth and nature. One of the things our history has served up is a rendezvous between man and nature, the most spectacular instance of which in latter days is the threat of nuclear holocaust and omnicide; more immediately, the reality of the degradation of natural environments. Surely we cannot any longer continue the nineteenth-century discrimination between spirit and nature, delivering the former to the humanists and the latter to the scientists, with never the twain to meet.

From my remarks on home and homelessness a thesis will emerge. It is that a fresh settling in the specificity of nature affords the potentiality of a human home for human homelessness, and thus a religation of the multiple locatives of human being. Modern man, said Matthew Arnold, is man deprived of "the last enchantments." I shall proceed by meditating three such enchantments, three rudimentary nouns in our language and the verbs cradled in them: *religion, nature, home.*

The pondering of these words that follows will be assisted by two brief prefatory observations, one about nouns, the other about etymologies.

37

One can only lament that grammar and ontology are not taught as companion subjects to our students from a tender age. Consider the noun and the verb, the union of which forms the simplest sentence. The noun names something, while the verb names an activity the something engages in or a characteristic the something possesses. The verb is the more fundamental because it names the manifestation, the way the subject appears. Thought that is to be free of immediacy does require nouns: the substantive names what moves from context to context without ceasing to be itself (John runs, John eats, John laughs: it is still John). But the verb is never context-free as connected with a subject noun: John is manifested as running, eating, laughing. Without the verb nothing concretely is manifested. We should remember that "the distinction between nouns and verbs, with the corresponding differentiation between a concrete situation and elements in it that can be found elsewhere, is a late development in language." Indeed, well into the development of European languages, the verb alone "can serve as a miniature of the whole sentence if it acquires personal inflections in its structure as in the Latin *scribet*."[4] Without the noun the verb names an anonymous manifestation; without the verb the noun names something not contextually manifest. No noun totally bereft of verbal undertones and overtones names anything. The clearest instance of the primordial coincidence of nominality and verbality surviving in our grammar is the gerund; and it is a good first ontological step to realize that the noun "being" is always properly a *gerund*.

In any case, if our three words (*religion, nature, home*) are *merely* nouns, if they are totally sedimented verbs, they are indeed the *last* enchantments and not worth the pondering. I do not think they are so sedimented; the great words in the language have a life of their own—even their concealing is a form of disclosure. What will claim our attention in meditating each of these nouns is their prenominal resonance, that verbal activity cradled within each of them which, could it but be made contemporary with the "right" context, would be kissed from toad to prince. We will make our meditation, of course, through language. It is not as though we might surprise that prenominal activity in the buff, without nouns, without sentences, without language. Our being as human being in the world is deeply, ineradicably a syntactic being.

I would seek, then, to stimulate (even if I cannot instantiate) the imagination of the verbality of the noun, the imagination of religion, of nature, of home.

A final prefatory remark about taking a reading on these words, initially, by recourse to etymology. One knows as well as the next person in the university that classical philology is on its last legs, done in by linguists and philosophers who contend that the meaning of a word is nothing other than how it is used (currently). But the question is, How do we get from one context to another? Clearly, we do so linguistically, and through *some* words that survive the transfer. In recourse to etymology for an initial disposition to the prenominal activity of these nouns, I align myself with such a humanist as Owen Barfield and such a historian and philosopher of science as Gaston Bachelard. Barfield (in such books as *History in English Words, Poetic Diction, Saving the Appearances*) has looked to rudimentary words as carriers of the correlation of consciousness and phenomena, as Bachelard has looked to like words as correlated with the elements of nature.[5] And so, in addition to the companionship of ontology and grammar, one admonishes and aspires to practice the conjunction of ontology and semiotics.

Religion

The English noun *religion* has two verbal roots with a common stem. Classical Roman thinkers derived *religio* from *religere*; the Christian Fathers derived it from *religare*. In both cases the central stem is *lig-* (*ligere, ligare*), which suggests "binding."[6] This sense survives in such English nouns as ob*lig*ation, *lig*ament, *lig*ature. It was a sense still evident for Gladstone in the third quarter of the nineteenth century when he condemned "religion . . . with a debased worship appended to it . . . but no *religating*, no binding power." If one takes this classical sense of Roman civil religion, religion means scrupulous attention to what claims and binds, to what holds us together (personally and socially) and obliges us to the source or sources of ultimate sponsorship in the world.

If one adds to the classical Roman the special sense of the Christian Fathers, above all that of Augustine, attention is called to the *repetitive* and *changing* character of ligation as the essence of religion. It is not binding alone or simply, but loosening from former bonds and re-binding, *re*-ligare, that is at the heart of religion. Religion that does not stop religating involves a combination of binding and freeing, of the fixed and the variable, of the same and the different, of the one and the many. To the classical sense of binding is added, in all three of the surviving Western religions (Judaism, Christianity, Islam), the religative significance of *time* and *memory*. Since selfhood is given in concert with time and memory, with space and place, we can say, in a reversal of the French adage, that the more things are the same, the more they are different.

In his *Confessions*, the first rudimentary autobiography and document of self-consciousness—in the modern sense—in the Western world, Augustine lays out the "binds" in which he has found himself. The mere knowledge of these binds—with the Manichees, his mistress, his bastard son Adeodatus, his pious mother Monica, the stealing of pears as a youth—was not religious. Not one's knowledge but what one *ack*nowledges (confesses: *confiteor*) is the stuff of *re*-ligation, of one's religious story. Long before Max Scheler, Augustine recognized that there is no possibility of forgiveness or salvation if the past is fixed. For Augustine the past is not bound but is subject to re-binding as one's story unfolds, folds out, and folds up in the coincidence of past, present, future. What seemed binding in the past proves for Augustine in the course of mnemonic probing not to have been so, while many trivial events in the past show themselves, in concert with an accumulating selfhood over time, to be provident. What one was *negligent* of shows itself as *religent*, as affording religation. In his and in every human memory, Augustine saw occasions neglected for their providential power. What these occasions provided (providence) were obliging surmises or evocations which now, through re-ligation, become invocations. Thus in a re-ligated life, the repressed never loses its pertinence to what may be obliged, and what is obliged is not to be formulated apart from what has happened—and continues to happen in the ligaments of story.

Religion, religating, so understood makes for an intense interior dialogue, a coincidence of opposites, a relentless tension between the elements of historically placed selfhood. Such a tensioned dialogue is conducted, for Augustine, in the presence of One who is absent to our surest speech and audiently present to our negligence. Religation, our tensioned acknowledgments, is an unending effort to know even as we are known by One who will not let us rest in the binds of fate. The temptation of the human heart is to rest in its own identities and identifications. Because religion *ligates*, it makes for duty, the fixed, the conservative; because it *re*-ligates, it makes for release, change, radicality. The temptation of religion in the West, often historically realized, is to split the tension between these tendencies, becoming either radically conservative and thus the ideology of a status quo or a status quo ante (as in today's American "Moral Majority"), or radically anarchic and thus the ideology of an avant garde (as in various forms of mysticism in the West, and in modern "liberalisms"). Religion with real religating power is shot through with dialectic: it is at rest and restless, at home and homeless, bound and free.[7]

Home

When one uses the word *home* he gives to it a valorization almost as unique as his own body odor. We cannot pause over *home* without an agitated reflexiveness, for it is accompanied in speech by a private onrush-uprush of *images*, what Bachelard called "sudden saliences on the surface of the psyche." Few words so steadily reflect their reflexivity, so immediately betray their imaginal peripheries, so directly embody the wistful or the alienated. In its unstudied utterance there is an idiosyncratic variation in which the cradle of the body rocks all sound. The catch in the throat, the sigh which carves the breath, give to *home* its tonality, its sonority. It is one of the few words left in our language in which the memory and the imagination of the body interdict all calculation. We can perhaps see why by looking to the primal verbal activities which the noun comprises.

The English word *home* is of Teutonic origin, and back of that there are probably Indo-European (*Em* or *M*: connoting "mine") and Sanskrit (the mantric *Om* or *Aum*) roots. And as a noun *home* is a compact of the reverberations of several Germanic and Old English verbs. There is the sense of Old Prussian *keimen:* to germinate; split the seed; be separated from the universal stock in one's own place, soil, and blood; thus to arise, start, begin in one's radical individuality. That sense pervades the German noun *Heimat:* the place of nativity, where things began, and where one fundamentally is *settled*, where one dwells, the *geography* of one's founding imagination. To settle, however, is not merely to dwell in, merely to inhabit. The Middle English verb *dwellen* (like Old High German *twellen*) adds another nuance: to intercept, to hold up, to stay, to tarry; so home is not only a place one dwells in, but also a place of dwelling on. That dwelling in and dwelling on is further amplified and racinated in the Old English verb *abidan*, which means both to go on being and to await, to "bide the time" expectantly, and so pertains to an abode one can or cannot abide. Finally, the Latin *residere*, to reside, suggests not only to settle or sink, but to be inherent in, to vest, to belong. To reside is not alone to domicile, but to settle down to what rises up as an initiating, originating, intrinsic claim or bond, a cumulative and aggrandizing *residuum*.

There are certain reverberations in the word *home* that chime with those in *religion*, and one may call attention to them even in advance of bringing the word *nature* into listening range.

We have seen religion to comprise a sense of ligation or binding, and have found a like sense in home as the place in which we inhere, in which we are vested, which claims us. We have further heard religion to comprise the sense of *re*-ligation, the loosening of bonds that cannot accommodate rebinding, as we have heard in home a starting that continues, a dwelling that dwells on, a founding imagination that accommodates an expanding residuum. To get a tap root down, and thus a plant, the seed must split (in something like the current vernacular sense: when we get away from here, we "split"). Man or woman is not a plant, however. The original place, however formative, cannot accommodate the perduring human home. Because ligation, to remain binding, to make present what is obliged, requires an unending re-ligation, one is driven from home into uncharted homelessness, from the domestic into the wild. Man, as H. Richard Niebuhr once observed, is like a migratory bird: he cannot be all that he is in one climate, one place. There is a doubleness, a multiplicity in his locative ground.

It is not by accident then that the "religious" in the world's religions have been at home in homelessness, have made home and homelessness to coincide. Peripatetics, wanderers, wayfarers, vagrants, mendicants, saunterers. All holy walking, said Thoreau, is sauntering.[8] The saunterer, he said, is the *Sainte-Terrer*, the one on the way to the Holy Land. Thoreau himself

42

was such a one; his errand into the wilderness was to find a home for his homelessness. It was in that sense that he believed "in Wildness is the preservation of the world." We should remember that before our American foreparents were settlers they were Pilgrims. The dialectic of home and homelessness in American Christianity has been thematic from the beginning: the dialectic of the uprooted and the rerooted, the uprouted and rerouted, the unligated and the religated. (A Roto Rooter-Router school of theology?!) And not only from *American* beginnings. The anonymous author of the Letter to Diognetus in the second century enjoined the Christian to make of every foreign land a homeland, and of every homeland a foreign land.

Parenthetically one may refer to *the* great philosopher of home in the twentieth century, Martin Heidegger. For him estranged, alienated, vagrant man is in quest of home as *dwelling*. For the American, however, and I believe this owes in some large measure to his or her experience of nature, home must embrace the dialectic of home *and* homelessness, the canny and the uncanny, the domestic and the wild. If Thoreau counseled settling down through the alluvion that extends from Paris to Concord, below freshet and frost, to rocks in place, where one might set one's Realometer, it was not merely to dwell or abide there, but to have as well a place one could get the hell away from, and awake in different climes. Only with such a place and only by leaving it, only by being simultaneously at home and homeless, can one dwell *on* the abiding abidingly.

It will have been noticed that I have not developed the dialectic between home and homelessness in one of the classical Western theological ways, by resort to this-worldly and otherworldly categories. When Western theology has been pressed into the use of those categories, it has been by reason of the hegemony of time and history as the framework of religious consciousness. It is otherwise with religions (including Christianity) that have not lost their ligations and religations with nature. Religions that are staked in nature—as Heidegger says, that preserve the earth, receive the sky, await the divinities, and escort the mortals— such religions have no need for a bifurcation of worlds to account for an inner-world reality. For *other* American foreparents (and mine), the American Indians, the house is the home of homelessness: the lodgepole or the smokehole opens the way for movement between planes, for the ascent and descent of the migratory, multiply located bird that we are.

Nature

In these last comments we have begun to trench on our third noun, *nature*, and we may now bring its verbal resonance into range. Etymologically, nature derives from *natus*, past participle of *nascor*, to be born, to be begotten. Nature then is the whence of things aborning, of things coming to be—and, by extension, of things decaying and passing away. Nature, then, is *genesis*.

It is a grievous lack in what I have said about our three nouns that so little account has been taken of the history that prevails over our hearing of them. That lack cannot be rectified in a few sentences, but I risk a few observations on the history of *nature*.

Before the rise of modern mechanics in physics and Enlightenment deism in philosophy, nature was understood on an organic model, as a living organism. Nature was the *creative* effect of intelligent soul, whether in mythological expansion that intelligence was understood, as in Christianity, to transcend the cosmic body, or to be embodied demiurgically *in* the cosmic animal, as in Greek natural philosophy. In both cases nature was not a *self-conscious* creativity because, as Plotinus said, nature lacks imagination: it cannot transcend its own becoming. The creative and creating effect of intelligence, nature cannot *be* intelligent. An intelligent, self-conscious rendering of nature's creativity is precisely the charge of human culture. Only a human culture unreligated to a nature so understood could forget a maxim that was unquestioned over two millennia of glorious cultural achievement: "Art imitates nature."

In early modernity, in a sea change of paradigms both for science and cosmology, nature is seen as the *created* (not creative) effect of an Intelligence that is not only remote but retired. "Creativity" becomes a buzzword in the language in respect of humankind. As the cosmos becomes centered on the sun, creativity becomes centered in man (who is at best an imitator of superannuated deity). Creativity is delivered into human hegemony and is exercised upon nature as its all-encompassing stuff. Present the stuff of regularity and absent the Regulator, man is usufructory creator. Omitting many important steps, we can see the apogee of this view, philosophically, in Fichte. For him, nature is the realm of the Not-I and exists as the counter against which the reality and self-consciousness of the I are shaped. In the very ecstasy of the differentiated ego, Fichte exclaimed: "I do not exist for Nature, but Nature exists for me."[9]

I shall bring these brief historical observations to a head with some comments about a genius of the first rank who negotiated the paradigm changes between the Enlightenment and the nineteenth century, and who anticipated their issue in the twentieth. Goethe was perhaps the last towering figure in Western culture to make signal contributions both to letters and to the sciences. He identified and deplored the split between spirit and nature that emerged in the nineteenth century, and the consequent dichotomy between the "two cultures" following on the assignment of spirit to the humanities (*Geisteswissenschaften*) and nature to the sciences (*Naturwissenschaften*). Attracted as they are to mathematics as their fundamental language, the sciences would lead to a quantification of all qualities and thus to an alienation of man from nature as concrete process. As for the romantic humanities, their energies would be siphoned off to feed "the hot paroxysms" of the human heart, unnourished by the amplitude of a nature rich in self-diffusion.[10]

While *Faust* stewed on the back burner of his mind for sixty years, Goethe entered the scientific lists and did experimental work in botany, anatomy, biology, and the optics and physiology of color. In something like the classical Greek sense, he was out to "save the phenomena" of nature. What would become of man alienated from the concrete experience of nature, estranged from the very geneses that nourish his or her life? The fundamental phenomenon, the *Urphänomenon*, was metamorphosis (a word Goethe introduced into the language), that morphogenesis by which "nature is constantly creating new forms. What now exists, never was before; what was, will never come again. All is new, and yet always the same."[11] In explanation of unity within nature's variety and change within her continuity, Goethe was an evolutionist nearly eighty years before the appearance of Darwin's *Origin of Species*.

The phenomena of genesis everywhere exhibit two irreducible principles, for Goethe. The first of these is polarity (*Polarität*). Every concrete phenomenon in nature is an interplay of tensions, a coincidence of opposites, a fusion of centrifugal and centripetal tendencies. The same polarity is at work in the arts and all affairs of the human heart. In his poetry and drama and novels Goethe ceaselessly alternates between the images of *Wanderer* and *Hütte*, man who roams and philanders, man who longs for home and family: at home and homeless, bound and free.

The second principle of nature's geneses is *Steigerung*, an all but untranslatable term. However much "polarity" accounts for unity within change, the one and the many, the same and the different, it cannot account or be responsible for the creation of new genetic forms in which there are *changes of quality*. *Steigerung* is that "intensified heightening" which gives rise to a new term, and thus to a new round of polar relationships. The same principle is at work in the arts. The justification for a work of art is that it establishes the human spirit at a new level of quality: nature and culture remain in tandem only as the *geneseis* of nature chime with the *poieseis* of spirit. And Goethe contended against the romantics generally, and Schiller particularly, that such a *Steigerung* is not a matter of "idea." Because heightening in nature is a matter of concrete fact, science is inescapably experimental and empirical; because heightening in the human spirit is a function of individual stories, Goethe tells of roaming and homing in connection with the *realia* of Wilhelm Meister's life, he tells of Faust and his dog. The tendency to become specific (*Spezifikationstrieb*), the tendency of all becoming (genesis) in both nature and spirit, which shows itself when nature and spirit are ligated and religated, is protection against the unhappy consciousness of the bad infinite (to use Hegelian language. And if *Polarität* and *Steigerung* sound like Hegel's *Dialektik* and *Aufhebung*, that is because he got them from Goethe). As Goethe suggested in *Wilhelm Meisters Lehrjahre*, "If we can believe it possible that the Creator of the World took upon Himself the form of what He made, and for a time lived with men on earth as *they* live" we can only revere the specific in both nature and man.

How Shall We Dispose Ourselves to Nature Religatively?

Earlier I called attention to reverberations in the words *religion* and *home* that chime with each other. From what has been adduced from *nature*, it will be clear that that word emits echoes which join the chorus of like resonances: to homing and roaming, to ligating and re-ligating, add from *nature* the ceaseless polarity of contraries and their intensified heightening in the quality of everything aborning. To be held in the embrace of nature, as we just now noted from Goethe, is to be joined to the specific (i.e., to what is manifest, what is phenomenal, what shows itself, or appears). And so I come to a thesis, that a fresh settling in the specificity of nature (scarcely the same thing as "a natural setting") may afford a human home for human homelessness and thus a re-ligation of the multiple locatives of religious sensibility. This thesis arouses two questions to be taken up in conclusion. *How* shall we dispose ourselves to nature religatively? And if we do, *what* are some of the re-ligations that might ensue?

First, then, how shall we dispose ourselves to nature in its religating potentialities? Not, as Goethe warned against the romantics, in hankering for the primitive, as though we had or could shed our civilized hides. There is an irony in Thoreau's admonition to get our feet out of the cultural alluvion of Paris and Harvard College, while he sits on his pumpkin at Walden reading books in Greek and Latin! If we are lucky enough to meet the raw, it will be from the standpoint of the cooked. An original innocence is closed to us; we are at best suppliants of a second innocence; in Paul Ricoeur's phrase, suppliants of a "postcritical naiveté." That means we cannot ignore *that* and *what* we know, and so we cannot follow Goethe in excoriating the sciences of the day (unless, like him, we can do them better). But we can aspire not to ignore that and what we do *not* know, knowingly. When humanists knew what they were about, they trafficked in learned ignorance (Nicholas of Cusa's *docta ignorantia*).

Let us revive an old idea: that the religative potency of nature awaits our being disposed to it as to a *text*. A text which invites our audience again and again is one which expands our learned ignorance. In developing the venerable notion of disposing ourselves religatively to nature as text, I am conscious of drawing explicitly upon Goethe and Thoreau (to their horror, one could add Calvin, though I do not).

Said Goethe: "To be enjoyed, to be turned to account, Nature herself must be present to the reader, either really, or by the help of a lively imagination." The phenomena of nature reveal and conceal themselves as a text, in the first instance,—partly as they appear unsought, partly as they may be presented by

47

contrivance," that is, by human culture.[12] In a paraphrase of Italo Calvino's paraphrase of Descartes, we may say that nature expresses itself as long as someone can say "I read, therefore it writes."

Thoreau went into the woods to transact some private business in nature's public. He traveled light, with only a few classical texts at hand. But his attentiveness discovered him in a vast circulating library where sentences were written in bark, where "much is published, little written," the source of sentences "merely copied from time to time on to linen paper." (Nature's motto: publish or perish!) In such a circulating library words might indeed be "nailed to their primitive senses" and the *poieseis* of human culture be replenished with the *geneseis* of nature. So Thoreau:

> A town is saved, not more by the righteous men in it than by the woods and swamps that surround it. A township where one primitive forest waves above while another primitive forest rots below,—such a town is fitted to raise not only corn and potatoes, but poets and philosophers for the coming ages. In such a soil grew Homer and Confucius and the rest, and out of such a wilderness comes the Reformer eating locusts and wild honey. . . . Alas for human culture! little is to be expected of a nation, when the vegetable mould is exhausted, and it is compelled to make manure of the bones of its fathers. There the poet sustains himself merely by his own superfluous fat, and the philosopher comes down on his marrow-bones.[13]

Without nature's *genesis*, human *poiesis* is bereft of religative nurture.

Well, then, if we are to be nurtured in the *re-ligative* potencies of nature, we are to be disposed to it not only as text but as a text of a certain kind. We are as postcritical persons to be disposed to nature as to the text of poetry. It is not as sheer genesis, the matrix of becoming and passing away, that nature presents itself as a text fraught with religative potentiality. (Without poiesis, nature is in bondage to a saturated discourse). Only when *genesis* is met by a commensurate *poiesis* does such a text emerge. Only then does space afford an alveolic place that can rebind us, one in which we are obliged to settle, dwell in and dwell on. In such a meeting of genesis and poiesis the tropes of nature arouse our latent capacity for parable, and the migratory bird in us finds its nest.[14]

We should of course remind ourselves of the restraints of a hermeneutic of texts. I have not said that nature *is* poetry, not even (as perhaps in Schelling) that nature is *unconscious* poetry. The tropes of genesis that nature polarizes and heightens are those in which we are not complicit; at least, we are no more complicit in them than is any other natural force. If nature did not retain the lead in this respect, if it did not steal initiative in the text which emerges at the junction between its genesis and our poiesis, we would have nothing to expect from that text but our own projections. (We would have, as in romanticism, the psychoanalysis of nature.) When a text is honored as text, it sets a limit to velleity and arouses the imagination: as Bachelard says, we aspire to repeat its creativity and continue its exaggeration. What religative poetry does with nature is what poetry does with everything it holds in view. To follow Bachelard once more, "Poetry puts language in a state of emergence, in which life becomes manifest through its vivacity."[15]

What Are the Religative Potentialities of a Fresh Reading of Nature?

Our final question is, *What* re-ligations might we expect from such a reading of nature?

(1) We might expect to be rebound to *variation*, we might expect the potency for variation that lies at the heart of natural process to involve us in ceaseless rebinding. Nature like religion has its ligations; its continuities, regularities, patterns. Scientists as much as theologians and for the same reason have a conservative streak; they attend to these regularities as affording an enduring human home.

But the essence of modern science, for which "evolution" is only the code word, is that nature has packed its trunks with potentialities for variation. Being the matrix of genesis, nature embodies both of the fundaments of creativity, the need to limit and the need to keep options open. A human culture that attended to the religations of nature itself would be one in which culture's classical practitioners and guardians, the humanists, would pack the attics and basements of the university with potentialities for human variation. In such a university students might wander into the attics and basements and, as the young will, try on the clothes. Many a new life might be found in such play.

(2) Ligated to nature's religations, we would no longer be able to avoid *one* potentiality for variation, and that is the possibility, some would say the accelerating likelihood, of *nature without humankind*.

One of the most fascinating and still unfinished chapters in the history of modern science is the resistance to an evolutionary theory of nature's religations. I refer not to the understandable resistance of some ("fundamentalistic") theologians, trapped in old ligations, but to the resistance of some scientists, repressing the same or similar ligations. Human terror lies at the base of this resistance. If species come and go, there is no reason to suppose man may not be among them; nature got along for millions of years without humankind and we must assume she could do so again. It is often claimed (as by Loren Eiseley) that this recognition and its regression account for the delay of the explicit formulation of the theory of the origin of species, a theory known to have hovered in the consciousness of scientists long before Darwin. And is it not the case that, having finally acknowledged an evolutionary account, scientists look to the stages of evolution in order to see how nature was teaching herself to make *man*—the scientific vindication of the myth of Narcissus!

In 1937 Eric Gutkind, a sadly neglected Jewish theologian and philosopher, questioned "whether man is, perhaps, a kind of blind alley of nature, into which the cosmos has run. Is man, perhaps, a kind of natural monster, destined to die out?"[16]

Have we begun to meditate the religations coincident with this potentiality, what some call this prospect? One who has, E. M. Cioran, opines in *The Fall into Time* that "one is never so much man as when one regrets being so." Because Western man is incorrigibly an accomplice of time and is afflicted with the awareness of it, he is tempted to exist in the Fichtean sense, so that all existence, even that of nature, is centered on his own. Yet the surprise of being in contiguity with nature is that "the surprise of being precedes the surprise of being *human* . . . it is less *natural* to be man than simply to be. We feel this instinctively: it is the source of our delight each time we manage to sidestep ourselves and participate in the blissful sleep of objects. . . . He who has never envied the vegetable has missed the human drama."[17]

In nature, if I may paraphrase Bachelard, something is always praying to be born. Were we attentive to nature, we might overhear what is praying to be born *after* man. What is praying to be born *in* man, that he or she may estop the interdiction of humankind that awaits humankind's interdiction of nature? I repeat: have we the surmises out of which we could rebound and be re-bound to such a variation, to humankind as marginal to the cosmos?

(3) A fresh disposition to nature would involve us in a religation of self-identity and self-diffusion.

It is often said (by Tillich and others) that man cannot evade the ultimate since that is his root concern. But neither can he endure the ultimate very long at a stretch, especially if "the ultimate" does not include him as he has come to perceive himself. If the Malthusian prospect is in large measure the result of human competition for an ever more individuated ego consciousness, we should be surprised only if the ego did *not* suppress and repress such a prospect and every other countervariation.

There can be little doubt that, in the West, time and history have afforded the medium of differentiation and individuation for man. Western culture, with rare exceptions, is the story of an accelerating repudiation of human anonymity, is the work of authors more than that of authorization, is a crescendo of rage for the signature of the unique. The passion for clarity and certainty which arose with modernity and which has persisted throughout its day was itself in the service of certifying the *ego* and its *sum*: clarity and certainty came to be the sum of its *sum*. Moreover, our very sociality came to be the founded in the shared complications of individual ego—hence the hegemony of Freud and Marx over contemporary social theory.

In a reversal of Eric Gutkind, we may say that as the "I" (or the Ego) was the aim of history and its latter-day Western civilization, so the "I am not" as a distinctively human potentiality lies in the lees of nature. However specific the religations of nature may be and are, with respect to individuality she is red in tooth and claw.

In calling for a religation between self-identity and self-diffusion as a distinctive *human* potentiality, it must be emphasized that this is a *re*-ligative potentiality. It is not that old ligation, that first solitude in mere animality from which we decline (and for which romantics pine). It conduces rather to a second and last solitude to which we may aspire and accede, one that carries the accumulations of the course through history. Practising ourselves in diffusion, we may be located in that last anonymity in which, through religations we cannot now foresee, we might find our signature.

(4) Juxtaposition with nature would involve us in a religation of proper selfhood and property.

The connection between "proper" (*propre*: one's particular ownmostness) and "property" is intimate. The ego and its competition for uniqueness is at the root of possession and property; property conduces to propriety. Nature too is miserly, discarding nothing that ever worked, but never to the end of individual aggrandizement. At the same time she is profligate in waste, in service of the total fund of variation.

What religations of religions themselves will be necessary if we are to enter nature and nature is to enter us with potentiating force? As the patrons of individuality, have not Christianity and Judaism, of course against their intention and will, made us frenetics of possession, fueling civilization with infinite desire, want, and need? Surely one of the doors nature opens to us is an apprenticeship in dispossession.

I am well aware how incompletely developed these potentialities for religation are as cited. And I may be told that it is a little precious to garner them by recourse to nature when one could get them directly by booking Pan Am to Banares or Kyoto. While it may be true that these potentialities have something in common with religions that hold a different view of selfhood and sustain a different relation to nature than those in the West, I believe there are crucial hermeneutical reasons why Americans cannot detour their own history in gaining access to them. In some deeply residual sense we are still what the Puritan Fathers and the Republican Founders called (in different senses) Nature's Nation, readers of the Book of Nature.

On this note we may turn once more, and concludingly, to Thoreau. He thought the passage over the Atlantic occasioned potentiality for the new American to awake in a New Creation, where one might "travel a great deal in Concord," climb the Mt. Ktaadns of the inward morning, and grow beans for the tropes they arouse in the parable maker. His inner compass pointed always west, his central metaphor for the home of homelessness and in which he saw the preservation of spirit and nature sourcing and sponsoring each other. Among his spare rations for the journey into wilderness were (in addition to the Western classics) the Vedic scriptures; he knew that if you go far enough west it becomes east. Should the noble American experiment fail, there is one more ocean to cross. *That* eventuality he viewed with mixed and troubled emotions: "The Atlantic is a Lethean stream, in our passage over which we have had an opportunity to forget the Old World and its institutions. If we do not succeed this time, there is perhaps one more chance for the race left before it arrives on the banks of the Styx; and that is the Lethe of the Pacific, which is three times as wide."[18]

Notes

[1]For the relation of early modern poetry to early modern science, see Stephen Toulmin, *The Return to Cosmology* (Berkeley and Los Angeles: Univ. of California Press, 1982). He treats of Donne pp. 217–36.

[2]*Thus Spake Zarathustra*, in *Nietzsche*, trans. Walter Kaufman (New York: Viking Press, 1970), pp. 125, 291.

[3]"But home I found nowhere: a fugitive am I in all cities and a departure at all gates. . . . I am driven out of fatherlands and motherlands. Thus I now love only my *children's land*, yet undiscovered. . . . In my children I want to make up for being the child of my fathers" (ibid., p. 233). "Never have I met the woman from whom I wanted children, unless it be this woman whom I love: for I love you, O Eternity" (ibid., p. 340).

[4]Robert Sokolowski, *Presence and Absence: A Philosophical Investigation of Language and Being* (Bloomington: Indiana Univ. Press, 1978), pp. 12–22. This work is a model study of the relation between grammar and ontology.

[5]Bachelard's view of the relation between language and nature, between things and valorizing imagination, is far too subtle and intricate to elaborate succinctly. For the theoretical foundation the reader may be referred to his *Poetics of Space*; for particular "elements," such books as *The Psychoanalysis of Fire, L'air et les songes, L'eau et les rêves, La terre et les rêveries du repos.*

For Bachelard, the history of science is unintelligible apart from the history of the imagination. Things are things by reason of the imagination's valorization of them. Attend to a "thing," which already is to valorize it, arrest its verbality through the suggestion of an adjective, and you have a substantive forthwith. This precisely is not the assignment of a *value* to a thing substantiated without imaginal complicity. It is in this sense that Bachelard says "Valorization decides being." Imaginal valorizings, or more simply, images, are thus the origin, not the product, of consciousness; formally construed they embody the dialectic of the inwardness of substantives and that of the psyche.

Modern man is distanced or alienated from nature by reason of an arresting of the valorizing imagination. Modern science is not free of fault for this situation, for it has tended to work with images that are the *product* of a fated valorizing imagination (e.g., those images of and out of a mechanical model). These products are taken to be *facts* rather than the residue of former valorizations; or they are taken as "values." There is much talk in so-called humanistic education these days about "prioritizing" these "values," as though such an enterprise would solve rather than instantiate the problem.

[6]These are of course matters of continuing scholarly debate. The common stem aside, Marie-Louis von Franz has recently pointed out that *ligare* and *ligere* have distinguishable and perhaps distinct meanings. She points out that in common parlance *ligere* meant "to pick up" or "to collect," as in picking up or collecting wood, or "to read," as in gathering up or putting together individual letters (*Alchemy: An Introduction to the Symbolism and the Psychology* [Toronto: Inner City Books, 1980], pp. 97 f.). I am grateful to Professor David Miller for calling this discussion to my attention. Yet I do not see that very much rides on this distinction, is gained or lost by insisting upon it. All grant that *ligare* carries the nuance of binding, tying, gathering together, connecting; and these nuances are close to those of *ligere*.

[7]Insofar as "religion" becomes a hardened, nondialectical ligation, and the scholarly study of religion is directed only to the substantialization of such ligations, I believe our departments of religious studies in the university or college might more honestly be called: The Department of *Negligious* Studies!

[8]Henry David Thoreau, "Walking," in *Walden and Other Writings*, ed. Brooks Atkinson (New York: Modern Library, 1950), p. 597.

[9]Johann Gottlieb Fichte, *The Vocation of Man (Die Bestimmung des Menschen)* (New York: Liberal Arts Press, 1956), p. 153.

[10]Erich Heller, *The Disinherited Mind* (New York: Meridian Books, 1969), p. 32.

[11]Johann Wolfgang von Goethe, "Die Natur" (Fragment), in *Goethe: Werke*, vol. 13, *Naturwissenschaftliche Schriften* (Hamburg: Christian Wegner Verlag, 1971), pp. 45–47.

[12]Johann Wolfgang von Goethe, *Theory of Colours (Die Farbenlehre)*, trans. Charles Locke Eastlake (Cambridge: M.I.T. Press, 1976), Preface to First Edition, p. xlviii.

[13]Henry David Thoreau, *Walden*, p. 617. These lines from Thoreau remind one of others from William Butler Yeats: "God guard me from those thoughts men think/ In the mind alone,/ He that sings a lasting song/ Thinks in a marrow bone."

[14]I have developed these cryptic suggestions more fully in "The *Poiesis* of Place," *Journal of Religion* 53, no. 1 (January 1973):36–47.

[15]Gaston Bachelard, *The Poetics of Space*, trans. Maria Jolas (Boston: Beacon Press, 1969), p. xiii.

[16]Eric Gutkind, *The Body of God: First Steps toward an Anti-Theology* (New York: Horizon Press, 1969), p. 136.

[17]E. M. Cioran, *The Fall into Time*, trans. Richard Howard (Chicago: Quadrangle Books, 1970), pp. 34–35, 52, 178.

[18]Thoreau, *Walden*, p. 608.

ROBERT P. SCHARLEMANN

3

The Forgotten Self
and the
Forgotten Divine

CRITIQUE HAS the double sense of negative judgment, as when one says what is wrong with something, and of self-analysis done with a view to determining the competence and limits of something. In the latter sense, Kant's critique of reason is a rational effort to judge the competence and limits of reason; a critique of religion would be a religious effort to judge the competence and limits of religion; and a metacritique would be an effort to judge our judging as such, be it rational self-judgment or religious judgment by another. A critique, in both its negative and neutral senses, always involves the making of a self-judgment. If we speak of critiques of modernity, then, we mean, basically, a modern evaluation of modernity, which is to say, a historical and constructive assessment of what modernity is, how it has arisen, what its components are, how it forms a whole, and where its limits lie. So understood, modernity can be said to be composed of at least three elements and probably also a fourth one: (1) classical antiquity, especially the Greek cultural and the Roman legal heritage; (2) Christianity, with its basis in Hebraic prophecy and Hellenic religions of redemption, and institutionalized in a sacramental and legal system designed both to absorb and to transform the natural and moral realms; and (3) the Euro-American shaping of the principle of autonomy which emerged with the Renaissance and the Protestant Reformation and which reached its maturity in the ethics of the Enlightenment. The period of modernity is one in which the third of these elements predominates over the other two, mixed with a fourth one as yet scarcely definable but noticeable as the more direct source of the industrialization and organization of modern society. It is a period that can be reckoned as having begun, in the West, with the fifteenth and sixteenth centuries, as having reached its spiritual maturity with the Enlightenment of the seventeenth and eighteenth centuries, and as having produced its technological offspring and the seeds of its own transformation in the nineteenth and twentieth. The speculative idealism of Hegel, Fichte, and Schelling early in the nineteenth century is a blend in which the Enlightenment reaches its fullest expression in the effort to recover, in the form of insight, the content first given in the form of unreflected images and in which, at the same time, the presuppositions of the Enlightenment are conquered. Dialectical theology and hermeneutical ontology of the 1920s, as well as relativity theory and quantum mechanics, seem to me to be postmodern phenomena. For they seem to represent a kind of thinking that no longer fits into the framework of Western metaphysics, which reaches its culmination in modernity in the split between subject and object. That is a framework which, briefly described, rests on the principles that the real is the positive, the unreal the negative, and that there is no third between them. These amount to the cosmological and metaphysical applications of the laws of identity, contradiction, and excluded third in formal logic. But this is a question that can, for our purposes here, be left open.

Critiques of this modernity embody, as one might expect, different types and different aspects of human concern, ranging from the technicizing of nature on one side to the privatizing of spirit on the other, with the conflict between industrialized labor and artistic work somewhere in between. Some of the critiques are variations on Spengler's theme, heard in volume 1 of his *Untergang des Abendlandes*,[1] that the works of the Western spirit— its science, art, morality, law—have increasingly alienated human existence from its natural vitality. Others are variations on a theme of the dialectical theologians, Barth and Tillich among them, that modernity is but the most recent chapter in the history of the disease that is human religiosity. "Alienation and illusion—that is the modern religion," wrote Jacques Ellul in 1975. "Should it [i.e., religion] be destroyed then? Ah! How simple that would be if it did not involve man! . . . To destroy those shelters, to close those escape routes, would be precisely to drive the great majority of people to insanity or suicide."[2] Still others have to do with the attenuation of spirit in the West, as when Heidegger, in his lectures of 1929–30 on the basic concepts of metaphysics, analyzed, as the basic mood of contemporary existence, that of boredom;[3] or as when Solzhenitsyn in 1978 asked in his commencement address at Harvard: "How did the West [all of a sudden] decline from its triumphal march to its present debility?" and answered his own question by reference to "the mistake" that is at the "very foundations of thought in modern times," namely, "the prevailing Western view of the world which was born in the Renaissance and has found political expression since the Enlightenment."[4] Further, there are critiques of the depersonalization that results from industrialization, from bureaucracy, from scientific knowledge, from technological merchandizing, and from electronic art.

Finally, there is the traditionalist, and sometimes but not always fundamentalistic, rejection of modernism as a threat to belief in the supranatural that is thought to be essential to the existence of the Christian church and to religion altogether. Thus, Santayana could write in *Winds of Doctrine*: "Modernism is suicide. It is the last of those concessions to the spirit of the world which half-believers and double-minded prophets have always been found making. . . . It concedes everything; for it concedes that everything in Christianity, as Christians hold it, is an illusion." Against such a modernism he set a "frank supernaturalism" as "the sole hope," the "sole dignity" and, indeed, the vitality of the church. It is not those "who accept the deluge, the resurrection, and the sacraments only as symbols that are the vital party," he wrote, "but those who accept them literally; for only these have anything to say to the poor, or to the rich, that can refresh them."[5] The theme here stated has many variations. But essentially the theme itself is that religion and modernity are fundamentally incompatible and that efforts to give modern interpretations of ancient religion are nothing more than the results of a will to have it both ways, which can end only in a compromise that saps religion of its vitality and integrity. Santayana's target was Catholic modernism—"modernism . . . is the historical attachment to his church of a Catholic who has discovered that he is a pagan."[6] But similar statements are made

57

by others as objections to Bultmann's demythologizing of the New Testament, Tillich's theory of symbols, and to any of the other ways in which the substance of a religion is said to be capable of being recast in modern form. They can serve here as a guide for delimiting the topic of the present essay.

Not all hermeneutical attempts have the consistency of Bultmann's method of demythologizing, which rested on an analogy and a distinction: the analogy that mythology was to the biblical mentality—as mentality and not as faith—the same as what science is to the mentality of the twentieth century, and the distinction between faith (as a response to what breaks in as different from any mentality) and any such mentality. But these hermeneutical efforts all do rest on the conviction that it is possible to distinguish religious substance from the forms in which it is expressed and to transpose that substance from one set of cultural forms to another set. Contemporary attempts differ from earlier ones to the degree that the distinction and transposition involve not just particular items—as might be the case when a translator must decide how to put basic biblical terms into a new language—but a whole. Bultmann insisted that the question of demythologizing was not a matter of adjustments here and there— as though one could dispense with the supranaturalist theory of miracles but maintain supranaturalism in sacraments—but a matter of a whole transposition. This obviously provides a greater difficulty than piecemeal translations. For there is no common frame of reference by which to judge the transposing, simply because it is whole. Hence, programs of demythologization or of modernism court denunciation more than do translations of sacred books out of their originals into other languages.

What gives this kind of criticism its force is, in part, that it involves the basic question of how the naive and the critical understandings of the world are related to each other. The force that supranaturalism has, even for the skeptically disposed who reject it for themselves while wanting others to hold to it, is due in part to its representing the first way in which one becomes aware of the realities to which religious symbols refer. The mythological-supranatural form of thinking, which is the characteristic of childhood, can also be thought of as characteristic of ancient cultures—so that one thinks of the ancients as having held, in adulthood, the forms of belief that today one associates

with one's childhood. This view gives to ancient culture a peculiar kind of authority—the authority of a childhood sanctioned
as such, the authority of a naive relation to the realities that are
presented in the religious symbols, or through the imagination,
a naive relation that is opposed to the critical relation produced
by the reflective grasp of the world of senses through questioning
and testing. Rejecting the supranatural or mythological forms
then seems to be tantamount to rejecting the truth one could
believe as a child but can no longer as an adult believe. This is
a matter that perennially divides the spirits, as it were, between
those who think of the childlike as an irrecoverable past, which
one inhabits before one becomes aware of how things really are,
and those who, on the other hand, think of the childlike as
representing the truth against the realistically perceived world
of adulthood. The spirits divide on the question of whether the
naive or the critical represents the truth of matters—the question
of whether one is closer to the truth when one can believe in the
world denoted by religious terms, stories, and judgments or,
rather, closer to it when one can no longer so believe. In this
quarrel, those who reject modernism and those who accept it,
both being convinced that modernism and religion are incompatible, have an interest in common; both want to see the issue
in the sharp terms of either/or—either the childlike as such in
its form, content, and meaning, or the mature as such in its form,
content, and meaning; either the supranatural and mythological
as such, or the scientific and *weltanschaulich* as such. Both parties
see in all modernizing efforts nothing but duplicity and deception, perhaps even self-deception. Even those, then, who reject
religion in this sense may still be interested in maintaining religion intact and not modernized. They may have, as it were,
grown out of their childhood, but they do not want anyone to
suggest that the form, content, and meaning of that childhood
were different from what, as children, they thought them to be.
When they speak of "traditional religion," accordingly, what
they mean is the religion which they learned as children and also
in the understanding of it that they had as children.

The alternative to this conception of the choice is, today,
hermeneutical theory, which builds on the confidence or, as Paul
Ricoeur likes to put it, on the "wager," that the naive can be
recovered in a critical form and that neither the naive as such

nor the critical as such discloses the truth of things but, rather, the naive when it is critically appropriated and becomes a second naiveté. Interpretation is, then, the passage to a plane of understanding which absorbs the naive and the critical in an act of appropriation, which can only be done through an act of the self as I. This is to say that contemporary hermeneutics stands, in a way, outside the issue of modernity and its critics. How that is so and what its significance is we shall defer for the moment in order to focus our discussion in the following thesis: *What gives the critique of modernity its force is a triple oblivion at the root of human existence in the West: the forgetting of being as such, the forgetting of self as I, who am not God, and the forgetting of the divine as God, who is not I.*

These three aspects of an existential amnesia, if one may so title it, are all symptoms of a single forgetting—forgetting that we can always already "understand." As the formulation indicates, there are three headings under which the emergence of modernity out of medievaldom can be placed. The first is that of forgetting the capacity of understanding, as something distinct from both perception and conception. It was the uncovering of this forgotten aspect that served to describe Heidegger's goal in the introduction to *Sein und Zeit*. For it is with understanding, and not with perception and conception, that the mind is first directed to being as such, rather than to concrete particulars of perception and to abstract genera of conception. Heidegger's whole opus from the 1920s might be read as a sustained effort to recall attention both to that capacity of understanding, which, though different from sensation and cognition, is as immediately exercised in one's normal existence as they are, and also to the correlative of understanding, the meaning of being as such, which, again, is understood as directly as individuals are perceived and genera conceived.

It is also a part of this same tradition of thought, however, to have forgotten that understanding the meaning of the word *I* and the meaning of the word *God* is the very act in which the question of the entities named by those words is settled because it is the understanding of the words that brings into actual being the ones they designate. That is to say, we cannot understand the word *I*, as we think or say or write it, without, in the very act, producing the one to whom the word refers. Kant pointed out the category mistake that is involved when, instead of recognizing what is thus meant by the word *I*, we discuss the question of the existence or nonexistence of an immaterial, immortal substance called "soul." Whether there is or is not such a substance is a question different from whether I exist and whether I as such have an eternal being or meaning. The two categories—that of I as such and that of an immaterial substance—had already been mixed by Descartes, when he slipped from the recognition "Thinking, I am" to the definition "I am a thinking thing." It is a slip easy to make, but making it illustrates the way in which the being of I was forgotten in the rise of modern thought. If, partly through the influence of Kierkegaard and the existentialist reflections on authentic selfhood (its *Eigentlichkeit* and *Jemeinigkeit*), the nature of this self-forgetfulness has become clearer, the same can perhaps not be said of the parallel oblivion of the meaning of "God," that is, the forgetting that, as with the word *I*, so with the word *God*, the act of understanding is the act through which the question of the existence or reality of God is decided. One cannot understand what one says or writes or thinks, when one uses the word *God*, without in the act pointing out the one meant by the name. One cannot invoke the name "God" without becoming the one upon whom the negative, the not-I, is shown; one cannot name God as an agent without thereby making the doer into one who shows God as the not-this-one of the action.

This, then, can be regarded as the heart of modern forgetfulness: not only has the objectifying habit of thought hidden the distinctness of the capacity of understanding, it has also hidden the way in which the very understanding of the meaning of the words *I* and *God* shows the reality to which those words refer, the one as the negation of the other.

The Forgetting of Being as Such

To speak of the forgetfulness of being is to pick up a theme of Heidegger, who never tired of emphasizing how thought in the West has become increasingly oblivious of being as such in its preoccupation with things and persons. I shall not here try to give a résumé or assessment of Heidegger's reading of Western thought; instead, I shall try to set forth the sense in which it seems clear that our habits of thought are in general those which overlook being. This will be a somewhat non-Heideggerian account of the Heideggerian theme.

What does it mean to say that we overlook or forget the "is" in such judgments as "This is a tree" and "The leaf is green" and "I am the one called N"? What it means can perhaps be seen most readily by reference to the way in which we usually conceive of the process of knowing anything at all—in short, by reference to our epistemology. We usually think of a judgment— such as "S is P," "This is a tree"—as composed of an abstract, general concept and a concrete, particular percept. The percept is the thing that we can physically see with our eyes; the concept is the abstract notion under which we subsume it, either as a common name ("tree") or as a generic concept ("a woody perennial plant with one main trunk"). The two parts to epistemological theory are, then, the perception of particulars and the conception of genera; every judgment unites those two elements. But what is left out of account is a third element, the understanding of being, that is, the undertanding of the meaning of the word *is*, in all its inflections, by reference to which the perceived particulars and the conceived genera are connected with each other. "Being" is forgotten in the sense that we consider perception and conception to give an exhaustive account of knowledge and leave out of account understanding itself. Thus, by way of illustration, the Aristotelian definition of truth as the correspondence between *intellectus* and *res* is taken to mean the correspondence between idea and thing, or between a mental picture and the sense-perception of a state of affairs. Instead, it is a reference to the correspondence between understanding and reality, in which "understanding" means not the thing either as thought or as perceived, but just the connection between perceived and thought object that is made when we say that something "is" something; "reality," similarly, means not the thing that is there but, rather, the connection between the thing as a perceived particular and a thought general which is expressed when we say that something really *is* what it is. Neither the thisness (the *haecceitas*) nor the what-ness (*quidditas*) is what is meant by "*res*" or "reality"; instead, reality is the connection between the this and the what, the particular and the general. Being appears in the mind as *understanding*, and it appears in the thing as *reality*. The term *ultimate reality* means, accordingly, the absolute connection in a thing between particular and genus or a subject and a predicate—it is absolute being in an object. The term *self-understanding* means, correlatively, the absolute connection of universal and singular in the mind—it is absolute being in a subject.

To the extent, therefore, that epistemology consists of a theory of perception and a theory of cognition but of no more, it is oblivious of the third element, being as being, which appears in part as understanding and in part as reality. But if being is neither perceived nor thought, how does it come into our field of knowledge, and what is its relation to perception and cognition? The answer, initially, is that being is the reality that is understood but neither perceived nor thought; and this is to say that the whole of epistemology is made up of perception, cognition, and understanding—three components and not merely two. But this does not yet answer the question of how the three capacities are related to each other. Traditionally, the formal relation of perception to conception is seen in the act of "subsumption"—the particular, which is perceptible, is subsumed under the general, which is abstractly conceived. The *act* of subsumption can be separated from the material in which it takes place, and that makes possible the development of formal logic. Formal logic has to do, not with anything in the real world, but with the possible ways in which subsumption can occur—either validly or invalidly, correctly or incorrectly. But if formal logic treats the act of subsumption as such, and if the act of subsumption is that of connecting the particular to the general, is not formal logic the very discipline that is involved with being— if being means the connection between particular and general? In a way, it is; but its very formality means that it is abstracted both from understanding and from reality, and is turned into calculation of formal signs, a transformation that becomes apparent in mathematized logic.

While this seems to suggest that there is something wrong with formal logic, such is not my intention. Formal logic as a discipline depends on the possibility of abstracting forms not only from material but also from understanding and reality, and thus of regarding the forms themselves from the point of view of connection. If the form of connection is subsumption, particulars are subsumed under genera, genera under still larger genera, until the most general of all, namely, being as such, is reached. The manner in which "being" appears in a logic of subsumption is, therefore, that of a highest genus, a universal in the form of the most general category under which all other categories are subsumable but which, in turn, is no longer subsumable. In a particular judgment, we can say, "This 'is' a tree, a woody perennial plant." In the most general judgment about the same particular, we say, "This 'is' a 'being.'" But we cannot go on to say what a being is. Being appears as a universal predicate which cannot become a subject. Does saying a thing is a being mean any more than saying it is something and not nothing? What is the significance of the outcome that both the most general thought and the most basic copula, namely, the "is" that makes connection between the particular and the general, bear the same name of "being"?

One way in which the forgetfulness of being becomes manifest is that this question—of the relation between the most general concept on one side and the object of understanding on the other side—does not get raised at all, to say nothing of getting answered. A possible answer is to say that the highest genus is not "being" but "something," for to say that a thing is a "being" ("This is a being") is to say, more exactly, that it is not nothing or, in other words, that it is something, without any further specification. The opposite of something is nothing; and the two terms are the two ultimates, related only negatively to each other— something is not nothing, and nothing is not something. This answer, in effect, points out a difference between the ultimate term of subsumption and the copula of judgments, despite the fact that in the metaphysical tradition they have tended toward the same name of "being."

This very answer would indicate, however, that being is indeed forgotten. That ·is to say, we would not make the mistake of treating being as a highest generic notion if we had not forgotten that the copula, the "is" that we "understand" but do not perceive or cognize when making judgments, is an element distinct from the objects of perception and cognition. The reason why we place "being" among the genera is that we do not know where else it might belong; and we do not know where else it might belong because we have forgotten the independent role played by understanding.

Recognizing that being is an object of understanding, but not of perception or abstract thought, does not of itself dispense with the question of knowing what being is. But this question must be answered by reference to the primary act of understanding, so that to ask what being is, is tantamount to asking what it is that we understand when we understand the word *is* (in all its conjugated forms). This turns reflection away from what is perceived and what is thought in the direction of what is understood, or, more concretely, in the direction of language. For it is in the medium of language that we understand, and it is in language that we find an objectification of what we understand. Language is the embodiment of being in the sense that it is to language that we look in order to see the physical texture of what we understand. The question sounds simple enough: What is it that we understand when we understand the word *is*? But a methodical answer to the question requires a reflection on language in the nature of a hermeneutics—a reflection which undertakes to put into correctly formed, ontological concepts the very same matter that, existentially, we always understand when we understand the word *is*. Hermeneutics was Heidegger's way of trying to recover, or to bring to attention, what was otherwise overlooked—namely, that what is meant by "being" is a matter that we have always already understood, so that our existential understanding is a testing ground for the concepts in which we try to grasp being.

Indeed, the beginning of ontology may be said to lie at that point when the word *is*, which otherwise is used to express an understanding or to show the world as what it really is, becomes an object of reflection itself; for that is the act in which one first tries to grasp reflectively what one unreflectively already understands. To say that a thing is a tree is to show it as a certain kind of thing. When we ask, however, "What is being? What does the 'is' mean?" then we have begun to think of being as such instead of understanding it as the background against which we think of other things. But one can forget being forthwith if one proceeds from that point to construe being as itself another generic object, differing from other objects by its eternal presence, its invisibility, and its other metaphysical qualities. This is a way of forgetting being because it leaves out of account that being is first of all what we understand and that, therefore, if we speak *of* being we are objectifying—making an object out of—an understanding. To remember being, by contrast, is to bear in mind that the objects with which we deal theoretically can be distinguished into three kinds: sensible, logical, and intelligible objects. As a percept, the object is concrete and sensible, located in a time and place; as a concept, the object is abstract and definable, not located in time and space. What is an intelligible object, that is, the object as an understanding, or as being? If as a particular, an object can be perceived with the senses; and if as a genus, it can be abstractly conceived; then as both of them, it can be understood. To know what we can perceive we turn to our senses; and to know what we think we turn to ideas; to know what we understand we turn to language. Put differently: to reflect on perception, we turn to our faculties of sensation; to reflect on conceptions, we turn to abstract thoughts (that can also be represented in diagrams and other abstract figures); but to reflect on understanding, we must turn to language, that is, to the realm of *signs* (or symbols), as distinct from both percepts and concepts.

To the extent that critiques of modernity are directed toward pointing out how current epistemology is often a symptom of the forgetting of being, they are in effect also opening the realm of signs (or symbols) as one that is irreducible to the realms of perception and conception. To be a sign or symbol is different from being a subject and also from being an object; and to be able to understand is to be able to see sense in signs (or meaning in symbols) through an act that is different from arbitrarily or conventionally attaching a subjective content to an objective material.

The understanding of being is our original dwelling place, the home that we inhabit and cannot but inhabit. When it is forgotten, it is replaced by images of the universe in which we locate ourselves objectively as a human kind among all the other kinds of thing. Thus, following Bernard Groethuysen (*Philosophische Anthropologie*, 1931), Martin Buber in his essay on philosophical anthropology entitled "What Is Man?" could chart the history of understanding in the West by reference to its *Weltbilder* and could put for modernity the question whether it is possible again to form a visual image of the universe in which human being can be located within the whole of being. For the ancient Greeks, Aristotle had brought to philosophical expression the visual image, derived from sense experience shaped under the dominance of the sense of sight, in which the human entity was one thing in a whole universe of things. As Buber put it, Aristotle was able to speak of man only in the third person, only as a specific thing among other things, in a universe seen as a space containing them all. With Augustine, seven centuries later and long after the collapse of the Greek cosmos, the utter homelessness of the human soul emerged, so that Augustine must ask the anthropological question in the first person ("What then am I, my God?"), even though the question is universal in that very person ("What is my nature?"). From the point of view of the question of understanding, one can say it is not by chance that Augustine opened again the realm of signs and interpretation. But in the post-Augustinian period a new house was built, a new visual image of the world was constructed, this time not out of sense experience of the world but out of the very experience of faith contained in Augustine's homeless soul. The new image, Buber remarked, was even more finite than the Greek; for it included time as well as space. The pattern in it was that of a cross: the vertical beam representing space, with the human heart just at the center, between the world above and the world below, and the horizontal beam representing time, with the crucifixion of Jesus at the very center, between the creation and the end. To be able to see man thus placed in a spatiotemporal whole was to be no longer homeless in the historical and natural world because the visual image was a projection of an original dwelling in an understanding of being. But because of the objectification in an image, Aquinas, like Aristotle before him, could speak of man in the third person, as a special part of the whole of things natural and supranatural. "[In] Aquinas, who was a theologian, and therefore in duty bound to know about the real man who says 'I' and is addressed as 'Thou,' that man speaks here 'as it were always in the third person.' "[7]

As this last quotation shows, the destiny of the *Weltbilder* is tied in with the second part of our theme, the forgetting of the self as I. Such world pictures, which are to be accepted not as fictional representations but as a kind of photograph of things, project onto a screen of objectivity not only the human habitation of an original understanding of being but also the consciousness of the self in its universal singularity. The picture was accepted as objectively real. "The Christian cosmos . . . was so real for every medieval Christian that all who read the *Divina Commedia* made in spirit the journey to the nethermost spiral of hell and stepped up over Lucifer's back, through purgatory, to the heaven of the Trinity, not as an expedition into lands as yet unknown, but as a crossing of regions already fully mapped."[8] Thus, if Buber's account of the role of world pictures is correct, as I think it is, then no confrontation with the self as I took place through the medieval image, because that self was the forgotten beholder of the soul making its journey through space and time. One needs to make one reservation to Buber's account. At one place only did this beholder, always in the background, come into the foreground: in the act of avowing or recanting a heresy. In enacting its capacity to be heretical, the self became a singular, eternally actual I.

Buber's account continues by noting that with the dawn of modernity, the picture is lost, so that the anthropological question reappears as a question posed in solitude, that is, by the homeless self, lacking either a theoretical image of its nature or a conscious understanding of its being. What broke the power of the medieval picture was the rediscovery of the infinity of space and time. "*Qu'est ce qu'un homme dans l'infini*—What is man within the infinite?" was Pascal's question. But now, Buber concluded, it is in principle no longer possible to form a picture of the whole because the infinite is not a whole at all. This conclusion is not refuted by the observation that we can indeed still make models or pictures of the universe even while recognizing that they are merely pictures or models. For in regarding them as merely pictures or as constructed models, we deprive them of the capacity to be real pictures and to provide the orientation that images of the universe provided. They cannot be taken as "given" in the same way that particular objects are "given" in the world. For that reason they cannot provide a real map for orientation. Hence, "the generation which works modern cosmology into its natural thought will be the first . . . which will have to forego the possession of an image of the universe; this very fact, that it lives in a universe which cannot be imaged, will probably be its feeling of the universe, so to speak its image of the universe: *imago mundi nova—imago nulla* [the new image of the universe—no image]."⁹ But what is an image that is not an image? Does not Buber's conclusion, too, point in the direction of the hermeneutical, the realm of signs in which things are what they are while signifying what they are not?

The Forgetting of Self as I

Buber's account of world pictures seems to reach the conclusion that modernity is a period during which the self in its solitude, far from being forgotten, is once more in the foreground. Furthermore, it may seem strange to regard self-forgetfulness as a mark of a period which is pervaded by individualism and concern with self-identity and in which the culture of Narcissism (Christopher Lasch) is as widespread as were the real cults of idols in days past. Would we not say, too, that one of the features distinguishing modernity from medieval civilization is the emphasis upon individual freedom and the rights of the individual? It is not the self in the form of the individual, however, that is meant when one speaks of the oblivion of self in the modern period. It is, more exactly, a matter of forgetting the being of the self as I that is parallel to forgetting being as such. But, again, does not Descartes, the inaugurator of modern philosophy, recover just that self in his famous proposition "I think, I am"? Yes and no. For one can see how deeply forgotten is the self as I in what Descartes himself makes of his proposition.

Descartes makes the discovery that when he undertakes to doubt everything methodically one thing remains indubitable, and that is the "I" of the one thinking. I can doubt the reality of the world by reference to how my senses can deceive me and also by reference to the possibility that I may be dreaming or that some demon may be perpetually deceiving me. I can doubt also that I am actually here. I may even undertake to doubt that I am even doubting at all. The activity of doubting can therewith shake my certainty of the reality of the world and of the nature of my own activities. It cannot, however, shake the certainty of myself, as becomes clear when I doubt my own doubting. For what remains certain in all of this is the "I" as such—that when I doubt or when I think at all, I am, surely. It does not matter *what* I think—whether I think I am deceived or not deceived by the appearances of the world, whether I think that I am doubting or not doubting. For no matter what I am thinking, the "I" who am thinking remains an unremovable point of reference. However radical it be, no doubt can erase the self-certainty that emerges in this way. When I think at all, I am.

Here is a new beginning in Western thought. What had theretofore been put into objective or generic concepts is now recognized for what it is—the original subject of thinking and of being; and what had been announced a century earlier in the *Hic sto*, the "Here I stand," of Luther's conscience, is now announced in the theoretical self-consciousness. Yet Descartes almost immediately "forgot" the discovery when he translated the thought "Thinking, I am" into the thought "I am a thinking being." This latter, by forming the concept "a thinking being," makes a kind of thing out of what had emerged as the "I," the self, of methodical reflection, and this transformation marks the character of modern, Cartesian subjectivity.[10] This is compactly stated in the second of Descartes's Meditations on First Philosophy: "I am—I exist: this is certain; but how often? As often as I think; for perhaps it would even happen, if I should wholly cease to think, that I should at the same time altogether cease to be. I now admit nothing that is not necessarily true; I am therefore, precisely speaking, only a thinking thing, that is, a mind (*mens sive animus*), understanding, or reason—terms whose signification was before unknown to me."[11] What Descartes discovered was that *when* I think, I am; he did not, however, discover that I am a thinking thing, and he could not have discovered it because I am not a thinking thing or any other kind of thing either.

How, then, shall we formulate what Descartes did discover? *How* am I I, if not as a subject set over against objects in a world? As with the forgetfulness of being, so also here it is by reference to language that we can explain the nature of the forgetfulness of self that was almost conquered in Descartes's meditation. He did not discover that I am a thinking being or that we are subjects existing in a world of objects. He did, however, discover the way in which the being of the self is connected with the word *I*. He discovered the linguistic phenomenon of *instantiation*, which contains the sense both of temporality and that of in-standing, the "when" of the Cartesian "I think" as well as the "here" of the Protestant "Here I stand." For what the word *I* does is to instantiate, to produce or bring about, an instance of what it means. No one can actually think or say the word *I* without in the very act becoming the one that is meant by the word. When I think or say "I," I become the one designated by the word. Descartes's certainty of the self amounted, then, to this: that the "I" as such comes to be at all with the word *I*—it comes to be when we think or say the word. The self as I comes into being with the thinking and saying of I: I am there, for me, when I *think* "I"; and I am there, for others, when I *say* "I." This self does not come into being as a perceptually distinct object—there is, perceptually, no difference between a human being who has not become a self and one who has. Self-consciousness emerges, rather, only with the appearance of the thought contained in the word *I*. This instantiating by the word *I* is in effect what is contained in Descartes's proof of the existence of the self.

The being of the self is, accordingly, not a connection between a particular percept and a general concept—as indicated in the proposition that I am a thinking thing—but rather the connection between the universal meaning "I" and the particular person who thinks or says it, a connection made by activating the word *I*. If so, understanding plays a double role here. It is, first, the capacity to see the meaning in the vocal sign "I." It is the capacity, in other words, to understand the word instead of hearing it only as a meaningless sound. Second, it is the capacity to understand one's own person as the presence of what is meant by the word *I*—the presence of subjectivity as such and not merely the location of subject. The being of the self is expressed, accordingly, not in the proposition "I am a thinking thing" but rather in the assertion "'I' am this-one-here," or, more simply, " 'I' am here," where "here" means the time and place of thought and saying. What defines subjectivity as such is not a generic concept but a place and time, denoted by "here." When I think I, I am; and where I am is here. Strictly speaking, therefore, we cannot say *what* I am but only when and where I am—I am when I think, and where I say, the word *I*, and then I am here, as this person.

To understand the meaning of the word *I* is to be as a self. Forgetfulness of self, like the forgetfulness of being, results from overlooking what we already can understand. If we overlook understanding, and confine epistemology to perception and conception, then we cannot take into account either being as the connection of particular and universal or the self as I. Being gets transformed into a metaphysical entity, a supreme subject or an absolute substance; and the self gets transformed into an immaterial soul-thing. That knowledge of the I is not of the same order as knowledge of things is recognized in Kant's conception of practical reason. Kant's operating principle was that we cannot expand our knowledge on the basis of concepts alone without intuitions. By that principle, we can have no knowledge of the self as transcendental subject—that is, knowledge of the I as such, as the originating point of all experience—because that subject appears only as a concept (in the thought "I") and is never given to observation. Whatever is given to observation is always presented *to* the subject-self but is never the I to whom it is presented, the infinitely recessive point of view from which all, including the empirical subject, is observed. Nevertheless, in practical reason—in the actual exercise of freedom—the I is there as a noumenal reality. In practice, to think "I" (in "I will" or in the resolution "I can" that responds to the moral imperative "You must") is to know the "existence" of the I—but only in practice, and that is to say, only in enacting the "I will" and "I can." That Kant could see the possibility of the self in the "I will" and "I can" but not in the "I think" may be due, biographically, to his Protestant upbringing; but it also is another symptom of the way in which the self remained forgotten in theoretical knowledge, for Kant did not clearly see how the unity of theoretical and practical reason lies in the understanding of "I" and how this understanding differs both from the *Verstehen* which he defined as knowledge and from the *Vernunft* that aims at the unity of knowledge in an infinite idea and ideal.

If a theoretical forgetting of the self is a hallmark of modernity, it means that we, as moderns, leave out of account that in the very understanding of the word *I* the self is there. A sign of this oblivion is that one tries to construct proofs for the existence of an immortal soul, or in some other way to determine whether there is a self that lives on independently of our persons. The basic fault with such efforts is that, from the start, they have overlooked that what is being treated as an object of proof or disproof is already there, present in the understanding of the word *I*. It is not the immortality of a soul that one seeks, but a reflective grasp of our understanding of the universality in the meaning of "I."

The self-understanding that is theoretically forgotten is not entirely absent, however; for what is theoretically suppressed may not only be enacted in practice, as with Kant, but also be symbolized in human works. From this point of view, Tillich's essay on the technological city, which was composed as an address delivered on the occasion of the opening in 1928 of the Leipzig exposition entitled "Die technische Stadt," shows how human works can be read as a language, that is, as a symbol, an embodiment of the understanding of being a self. Tillich offered an analysis of the technological city as such a symbol. Like every work, the city can be treated either as the thing it is or as a symbol expressing an understanding of being. To treat it as a symbol is to analyze it for what it might disclose about the way in which human being, in its psychical and social dimensions, is actually understood. What does it disclose?

Tillich proceeded to answer the question by reference to an original existential feeling of not being at home in the world—the feeling of the uncanny, the strange, the unfamiliar, *das Unheimliche*. For the response to feeling the uncanniness of existence is to try to protect oneself from it, and the preeminent symbol of how one understands that desire is the building of a house, which by enclosing a certain space shuts out the uncanniness of spatial infinity but which at the same time avoids the uncanniness of total enclosure by such things as windows and balconies and a surrounding yard or garden. The very building of a house shows how human being is understood—as the mediation between the unlimited and the totally limited dimensions of space. Human being is the mean in which the extremes are connected. As the house, so too the city and, eventually, the planet are expressions of such an understanding. The modern city, however, shows a difference over against the medieval, and through the contrast of the two we can see what modern self-understanding is. Buildings in which whole walls are windows and which have the heights of skyscrapers, streets that are broad and lighted, suburbs that replace city walls, these all show a drive toward the infinite to overcome an anxiety of the narrow.

Medieval towns represented the opposite: anxiety in view of the infinite and a drive toward the security of the enclosed. Modern cities, Tillich wrote, are "symbols of the conquest of restriction and narrowness" without, however, becoming victim of an infinite openness (*"Symbole einer Überwindung der Enge, ohne daß die unabgeschlossene Weite hereingelassen wird"*).[12] What is true of the house and the city is, in the end, true of the whole of technology: "The technical house, the technical city, the planet earth, controlled by the technical city and made into a human house: that is the symbol of our age, the age of the fulfillment of technological utopia, the age of the inhabitation of the earth and of the appropriation and transformation of the earth through human means?"[13]

That is, however, only one side of the modern self-understanding. The other side is that the very technology which was used to conquer nature and make one feel at home in the world threatens to take on a life of its own and to raise the question of who can control it. Out of these two sides of the understanding there arises a contradiction in understanding of the self: things have lost their mystery, their uncanniness, but at the same time the technological city has not become familiar or trustworthy. A new feeling of the uncanny arises out of the deadness of a world that, even while it may serve us well, cannot "speak to us as the living to the living." Hence, the technological city as a symbol discloses the question contained in modernity; it is, Tillich concludes, a symbol in which we can view our selves in the power and the questionability of our being.

To sum up: Theoretically, the self as I may be forgotten; technologically it is implicitly understood in the feeling that is built into the house, the city, the planet: the feeling of the self as the source of power for conquering the strangeness of nature but simultaneously the source of nature's death and of human alienation. What does that ambiguous feeling mean? Metaphysical proofs or disproofs of the existence of a soul provide no answer because they are symptoms of forgetfulness; for if one is aware that understanding is where we dwell, then the question of the self, like that of deity, is a question of how "I" and "God" are instantiated. Like the self as I, the divine as God can be forgotten, not least of all, perhaps, in religion. The question of their meaning involves the effort to grasp the creativity by which they come to be.

The Forgetting of the Divine as God

What ties together the oblivion of self and of the divine is that both of them involve the instantiating capacity of language. We said earlier that what Descartes discovered in his famous proof of his existence was the way in which the word *I* instantiates the self that it designates. The same is true of the word *God*, when God is understood as the divine that I am not and that is not I. This is not a distinction between God and my person or any other person. Rather, it is the distinction between God as the other of the self that is designated by "I." What we understand by "I" is not identical with any particular person, but is that universal meaning which is instantiated at the places marked by different persons and in the times when different persons think the meaning of the word. In thinking "I," I become a self, and I am here. In thinking "God," however, I become the one upon whom the not-I is shown. God is here, if one may put it so, as a negative presence—as the one I am not and the one who is not I, as the one who is not here but everywhere. Hence, to understand the meaning of the word is as such to become the time and place at which God is not. God's becoming has the form of negative in-standing.

With the introduction of the word *God*, the sign-relations undergo one more complication. We remember the self by understanding the word *I*; we remember being by understanding the word *is*; and the two are combined when we remember the being of the self in the thought "I am this one here." In the process, the word *I* is understood as a sign carrying the meaning of self, the "am" is understood as the connection between that meaning and this particular place and time, and this person that I am is understood as the sign of the presence of I. To understand the self—or to remember the I—means, therefore, both to understand how the word instantiates what it means and also to understand a person as a "word," that is, as a sign of the meaning of self; the unity of both lies in this that the person who says "I" is, when saying it, the Dasein, or the existence, of the self. When the word *God* is introduced, this self, of which the word is a sign, becomes in turn a sign of another, the not-I, which the self as sign can point *to*, but not point *out* except as a negative presence, as the one *not* here.

The question of the knowledge of God is, therefore, like that of being and of the self; for it has to do with a process in which an understanding is brought into reflective grasp, rather than with proofs of a metaphysical entity. Like proofs of the existence of an immortal soul, the proofs of the existence of God are symptoms of the forgetfulness of the divine that is already there in our understanding. They indicate that, because this realm, the realm of understanding, is overlooked, the meaning that is instantiated with the word *God* is transformed into the concept of a metaphysical entity whose existence may be disbelieved or believed. What is wrong with those proofs is that, like the proofs of an immortal soul, they start with the wrong question. They assume that what is at issue is whether there is an entity corresponding to the concept of God. But what is really sought in the proofs is, instead, the meaning which is always already in fact there in our understanding of the word and which is instantiated when and where the word is actually understood. The difference between the words *I* and *God* lies not in their instantiating capacity; it lies rather in the meaning that each instantiates—with the thought "I," the self is posited; with the thought "God," the nonself, the not-I, is posited. (This is, at least, the case from a critical or "modern" standpoint. It is possible to construe a circumstance in which the relation between the meanings of "I" and of "God" is just the reverse—that is to say, a relation in which "God" posits selfhood, and "I" posits the negative of it—God is all and I am nothing.)

Though he had nothing to say about the phenomenon of instantiation, Karl Barth did exhibit in his reading of Anselm's famous proof of the existence of God the turn toward understanding that seems to underlie critiques of modernity.[14] For he took Anselm's proof—which asserts, in effect, that no one can without logical self-contradiction both understand the meaning of the word *God* as, in Anselm's wording, "that than which a greater cannot be thought" and also deny that the one so named is real and not only an idea—as charting a route along which an unreflective understanding of the meaning of the word *God* is appropriated in reflective form; it is a movement of understanding what we understand. This is quite different from a procedure of trying to deduce necessary existence from a definition of God; for its starting point is not at all a definition of God but a statement of understanding. If one understands the word *God* to mean "that than which . . . ," then, by reflecting on that understanding, that is, on the meaning of the being of God as the connection of the word *God* and the limit to thought indicated in the phrase "than which a greater cannot be thought," one can see what it is that one understands. What one sees is that one already understands how the very naming of the word is the same as the positing of the reality named. The word *God* is to the presence of God what the word *I* is to the presence of the self; and just as the self becomes identified with the time and place of the person who thinks and says "I," so the divine becomes identified with the time and place of the naming of "God" as the negation of the one who does the naming. Tillich more nearly incorporates this aspect of the matter by distinguishing between the question that is contained in the proofs of God and the answer that is contained in the symbol "God." That is to say, Tillich's treatment seems to recognize the way in which the word *God* contains an understanding that both invites and defies proof; it poses a question of the unity of meaning and reality while not presenting that unity. To understand the word *God* is to recognize that the one meant cannot but be real but also to recognize that no reality corresponds to that understanding, and that is to say that the manner of the divine presence is that of a symbol— anything can point to, but nothing can be, the divine as God. God is God as that which no one and nothing is.

The forgetting of the divine is of a piece with the forgetting of being and of self. Like the other two aspects of the oblivion, it rests on overlooking the peculiar place that is occupied by our understanding, in contrast both to our perceiving and to our conceiving of the world, and is an aspect of the modern epoch. Modernity is often characterized as determined by a split between subjectivity and objectivity which carries with it the tendency to see the true and the real only in the objective and the impulse to use knowledge for the end of controlling the objective. As the theologies of secularity often pointed out when they flourished in the 1960s, the roots of this modernity may be traced to the biblical doctrine of creation. But the danger it harbors in the twentieth century comes from having dissolved the connection with that biblical doctrine. Thus Gogarten presented a theology of nature which saw modern secularity as a legitimate offspring of the biblical faith in God as creator; for that faith, by distinguishing in principle between God and the world, the creator and the whole of creation, brought about the possibility of human freedom from and for the world.[15] It is that faith which is historically at the root of the freedom whose chief bearer in the twentieth century is mathematized science and technology. The world could be cleared of its demons, of the belief that there are invisible spiritual powers acting as causes in nature, by the belief in the world as a creation, a domain given over as a trust to human control. But a domain that can be controlled is always only a part of a whole; it can never be the whole itself. This is exactly the recognition typical of secularity. Thus, the danger that modernity presents is not its secularity nor its will to control nor its objectification of the world, which are expressions of human freedom. Rather, it is that the basis of this freedom has been lost from view. In its early stages, modern science still presupposed, as self-evident, a metaphysical foundation, a philosophical-theological wisdom, from which "the big questions" could be answered while science devoted itself to its particular questions.

But the self-evident validity of the metaphysical answers has long since been lost, with the result that secularity is perpetually tempted to become secularism, and science, to become scientism, to make up for the loss. To Gogarten's view, these temptations raise a question parallel to Buber's question of finding an orientation in the universe. Who, or what, is to answer for the whole of things? To restore the metaphysical view is as impossible as restoring an image of the universe. The reason—though Gogarten does not so formulate it—is that in modern science the causal connectedness that articulates the world is, like time and space, infinite; and this is what is meant by the "closed causality" of the world of scientific observation. It does not have to do with whether causes are thought of as mechanical and deterministic or statistical and indeterministic but with the fact that the investigation of causes never becomes anything other than an investigation of causes. This is a respect in which modern secularity differs from its Greek predecessor. Because of that infinity, science cannot answer for the whole because the whole is unreachable; it can be a demand but not an accomplishment.

Yet without some answering for the whole, the character of science as science and as the bearer of secularity runs the risk of being lost. Gogarten sought to demonstrate this by reference to two basic qualities of scientific endeavor—its disinterested and its presuppositionless attitude. Science is ideally without any presupposition in the sense that neither its results nor its methods are ever exempt from critique and possible change; everything can be called into question, there are no infallible authorities. It is disinterested in the sense that it pursues the truth regardless of whether the truth supports social, political, religious, or other interests. But, while there are no external presuppositions or interests to which science is obligated, there are self-reflective limits to the absence of presupposition and interest. For science cannot be disinterested in its own possibility of being disinterested, and it cannot be without presupposition concerning its own being without presupposition. Yet since, strictly speaking, science as such cannot take an interest in its own disinterest or presuppose its own presuppositionlessness, it depends upon something else for the condition of its own being as science. If it tries scientifically to establish its condition as science, it inevitably becomes scientism, a pseudometaphysics replacing other metaphysics. What then can provide a condition for the possibility that science remain science and that it participate in the whole truth precisely by its self-restriction to fragments of truth? Gogarten's own answer was that science presupposes, as the condition of its being, faith in God as creator. That is to say, it presupposes the capacity to entrust the *whole* of things to the one who we are not and who is not we. If we say that the absence of such trust is due to having forgotten our capacity to understand the being of that one as instantiated in the very word *God*, then the conclusion of Gogarten's critique of modernity and his criticism of secularism are a repetition of the outcome of critiques otherwise.

This sketch of the oblivion of being in the modern world is not meant as a sociological description. Without empirical research, there is no way of knowing the number of people to whom the description would be applicable. But it is meant as an analysis of the dynamics at the basis of modern society and culture; and for that reason, it will be well to give some consideration to the question of what is portended by this situation—a situation to which the most daring theological interpretation is given by Thomas Altizer's recent work, in particular his book *Total Presence*.[16] In that book, he interprets both the anonymity of self that is characteristic of contemporary fiction and the death of God that is characteristic of contemporary nihilism as a completion of history: the self as I has so totally entered into our personhood that there is no longer a tension between the I as such and a particular subject, and the transcendent God has so totally entered the world that there is no longer a difference between what happens by nature or by human will and what happens by divine will. My summary here will be less daring, since it will be confined to a consideration of what is indicated by the turn from the metaphysical to the hermeneutical at the end of the modern age.

The Critiques of Modernity and the Question of Understanding

Historically viewed, this modern world emerged in large measure as a rebellion against the cultural unity of the Middle Ages that was based on the principle of absolute ecclesiastical authority. In some Western countries more than in others (in France, for example, more than in the United States), one of the results was a thoroughgoing anticlericalism and mistrust of ecclesiastical power; but in all of the countries, the modern world has been stamped by that negative relation to the medieval world, even when, as in the case of the Protestant Reformers and the Renaissance, the rejection of medieval authority was based upon what was thought to be the recovery of an earlier and more pure classical and biblical authority (the authority of the things themselves and of the word of God) rather than the formation of a new culture. One of the abiding features of modernity is, therefore, a negative relation to authority understood as authoritarian. The positive feature that stands as a counterpart to this negative one is the modern liberation of the individual person. For it is this feature that, in large measure, must receive credit for the success of the rejection of authoritarian culture. Nothing expresses its power more succinctly than Kant's definition of the Enlightenment as the achievement of a stage at which reason is capable of throwing off its self-imposed immaturity.

Other features of modernity are in part consequences of this basic rejection of authoritarian culture and in part apparently the result of new impulses not easy to recognize or define. It is possible to explain the modern totalitarian state by reference to the manner in which the state took on the functions of the church even while being conscious of its inability to take care of the inner or spiritual side of things that was also part of the unity of medieval Christendom; for totalitarianism can be viewed as the effort to repress one's consciousness of the state's inadequacy to deal with the whole of human reality. It is also possible to understand both the individualism and the pluralism of modern culture as a working out of the principle of freedom, and secular humanism as a result of the reaction against ecclesiastical domination. This is not to say that there is any single principle—whether it be anti-Christian attitudes, individualism, secularity, progress, or decay of ancient cultures—from which one could construe the whole of the modern world. It is to say only that the transition from medieval to modern has left as one of its general traits the antiauthoritarian. The principle of individual freedom, which, when combined with the regulation of things by reference to the most general concepts possible, is an overarching feature of contemporary states and societies and accounts for many of the specific traits; the technical control of nature and its application in capitalist economies; the recognition in theoretical, practical, and poietic reason of the autonomy of self-consciousness and conscience as a principle superior to external obligation; similarly, the rise of the independent sciences, sciences independent both of their philosophical and of their theological foundations—these, too, may all be seen as part of this whole rebellion and might be described as the positive shaping of the negative reaction against the unity of medieval society and culture achieved by the principle of absolute ecclesiastical authority. But other aspects of modernity seem to result less from a rebellion against ecclesiastic dominance than from the infinitization of reality mentioned earlier, or the reemergence of the power and principle of the infinite, as, for example, Alexander Koyré charted it in his book *From the Closed World to the Infinite Universe.*[17]

All of these things must surely be regarded as developments that one would not wish to undo. But this is not the same as saying that there are no dangers and nothing to be rectified in

81

them. Nor is it to say that we have not already in some major ways passed beyond the modern to something else. In a recent essay, entitled "Beyond the Modern Western Mind-Set" and published as chapter 8 in his book *Beyond the Post-Modern Mind*, which embodies a focused and slightly revised statement of the thesis in his earlier book *Forgotten Truth*, Huston Smith points out some indications of the postmodern.[18] The nature of the modern Western mind-set—for which Smith uses the rather inelegant acronym MWM—can be stated, Smith asserts, in a single sentence: "An epistemology that aims relentlessly at control rules out the possibility of transcendence in principle"; by transcendence, he means "something that is better than we are by every measure of value we know and some that elude us."[19] It rules out transcendence simply by virtue of its controlling character—nothing transcendent could ever appear to such knowledge because anything transcending control would not be part of what is knowable. "An epistemology that drives single-mindedly toward effective knowledge is not going to allow transcendent realities to exist."[20] It shuts out, for example, "the possibility of there being something that, better than we are in every respect, could infuse us with goodness as well as power were we open to the transfusion."[21] Among its assumptions are (1) that history can be controlled, (2) that happiness can be bestowed, and (3) that truth is instrumental.[22]

The mode of explanation which this kind of epistemology employs is a reductionistic one, in the sense that the workings of the higher things are explained in terms of the workings of the lower: "For Newton, stars became machines. For Descartes animals were machines. For Hobbes society is a machine. For La Mettrie the human body is a machine. For Pavlov and Skinner, human behavior is mechanical."[23] Smith finds no difficulty in assembling an array of quotations from contemporary authors to the same effect: Carl Sagan, for whom the " 'fundamental premise about the brain is that its workings—what we sometimes call mind—are a consequence of its anatomy and physiology and nothing more' ";[24] Francis Crick, who describes it as the ultimate aim of modern biology "to explain all biology in terms of physics and chemistry"; and others.

Smith criticizes this epistemology not because he wishes to disavow it altogether but rather because he wants to show that a failure to recognize its limitations is the root of the conflict today between the different centers of society and of the self. "While the West's 'brain,' which for present purposes we can equate with the modern university, rolls ever further down the reductionistic path, other centers of society—our emotions, for example, as they find expression through our artists, and our wills, as evidenced in part by rise in crime and senseless vandalism—protest. These other centers of our selves feel that they are being dragged, kicking and screaming, down an ever-darkening tunnel."[25]

The limits of this mind-set are indicated, then, when Smith goes on to say that it does not know what to do with mind: "We understand something of how the brain works, and, yes, through depth psychology something of how the mind works too. But when it comes to infusing the mind with motivation and meaning, the MWM is helpless. . . . [We] have abandoned the mind by converting to efforts to understand it in terms of things other than itself and lower than itself."[26] Smith concludes the chapter with a description of an approach to a different kind of cognitive outlook, whose aim is not to control but to participate in the world.

Instead of pursuing Smith's projection of a postmodern mind-set, I shall confine myself here to pointing out two cases that appear to my view to be clear indications of a postmodern mentality already at work: one is the formation of quantum and relativity theory in physics, the other is the formation of dialectical theology in the 1920s.

The development in physics is known well enough, in general outline, to make unnecessary an elaborate account. Relativity theory and quantum mechanics broke with Newtonian mechanics because the phenomena of subatomic particles did not fit into a mechanical model of objects and did not accord with the behavior of macrophysical objects. To be a wave and to be a particle are two different kinds of things in the macroscopic world, and yet the microphysical objects displayed qualities that made it necessary to think of them as being both wavelike and particle-like. Capra's *Tao of Physics*, which may be somewhat sensationalist, is one of a number of works to chart the development in somewhat popular terms.[27] Its significance can be stated in the observation that with the rise of this physics the discipline of

83

physical science must include in its account of reality the observing subject as well as the observed phenomena. This is an ontological dimension of physics, if "ontological" refers to a dimension in which there is a unity of subject and object, of *logos* (the measuring apparatus) and *on* (the measured realities). This is not ontological in exactly the same sense as is the phenomenon of understanding which appears in Heidegger's *Being and Time*,[28] for it does not resort to language as the medium in which the unity of being and thinking is presented; but it has to take into its calculations both the measuring subject and the measured object because there is no way of cleanly disengaging the observing instrument from the observed reality. Every experimental result must be read, accordingly, as a unity resulting from an interaction between the measurer and the measured. The line of demarcation between subjective and objective, which is the hallmark of classical physics and of the objectivity of the everyday world, cannot therefore be drawn. Microphysical reality seems, therefore, to have made visible a dimension in the physical world which has the characteristics of language. This raises the question of whether the subatomic realm is a dimension of reality not only like but also the same as the world that appears when language is created. Have physical instruments now uncovered the same realm as the one that language has always been uncovering? Regardless of how one answers such a question, it seems clear that this new physics is in some way postmodern—not only post-Newtonian but also post-Cartesian.

The emergence of the ontological dimension in physics has a parallel, if I am not mistaken, in the "dialectical" theology of the 1920s, associated with such names as Karl Barth, Friedrich Gogarten, Paul Tillich, Rudolf Bultmann, and others. While the new physics had to refashion its concepts in order to grasp a realm of reality in which the differences that prevail in the world directly accessible to sense perception and cognition do not apply—electrons are both particular and undular—dialectical theology refashioned its concepts in view of a metatheistic and even a metareligious realm—a realm in which the opposition between the I and the not-I as well as between the believer and the nonbeliever does not hold. The nature of this movement in theology is not very widely understood, and the label "neoorthodoxy" does little to contribute to the understanding. But the conception of Protestant preaching that Barth set forth in his essay of 1922 entitled "The Word of God as a Task for Theology" indicates what is involved in his transformed understanding of the word of God.[29] The obligation to preach is peculiarly constitutive of Protestant theology because preaching plays a role there that is comparable to the role of metaphysics in medieval theology: it is the arena of verification for theological assertions, whose truth or falseness depends on how they can be declared and heard. To preach is to speak in a discourse that is intended to be not merely the discourse of a self about this or that but in truth the discourse of God about God's relation to the world. To put it in Julian Hartt's words: "When the church preaches faithfully the rhetoric itself becomes representational: there is a place and a moment in it in which every hearer can begin to recognize himself."[30] The sense that this obligation to speak so is both necessary and impossible to fulfill was, in Barth's theology, comparable to the paradoxes of the new physics. How so? To Barth, the contradictory obligation was as baffling as were the experimental results to the physicists. That is to say, the obligation to a word of God contains an idea of a dimension of language that cannot be fit into ordinary discourse. In the ordinary meaning of the terms, God is the one I am not; and to say "God says" is to say the same as "Not I and not anyone else either says." Yet the word of God is that kind of speaking in which the difference between I-speaking and not-I-speaking is to be bridged. If what is puzzling about the subatomic phenomena is that they appear to be both waves and particles, and we cannot imagine what something that is both might be, then what is puzzling about the idea of a word of God is that it is a language in which "I say" and "I do not say" (or "Not-I say") are both applicable, and it is a discourse in which the true is also false and the false true. Judged according to the obligation to speak it (the "necessity"), it is true (it is a word of God); but judged according to the ability to do so (the "possibility"), it is false (it is not a word of God). This situation, in which what is said both is and is not a word of God, is the theological situation; and Barth summarized it by saying that theology must recognize both that it must and that it cannot so speak and, in acknowledging both the necessity and the impossibility, let God appear as God.

This principle of Barth's dialectical theology says, in effect, that one cannot draw a clear line between words which are a word of God and other words which are merely human words.

For, when one is dealing with the dimension of language indicated by the word *God*, then the distinction between the words which are of an agent and the words which are not of that agent cannot be sharply maintained. The word of God means a language which, when it is most my own saying, is not my own. Ordinarily, if I am speaking on my own, then no one else is also speaking through my words and voice; but if I am speaking as an emissary or representative of another, then I am speaking not on my own but on behalf of that other one. But in the theological situation, one is speaking in such a way that while speaking most on one's own, not bearing the message of another, another is speaking. In saying what one has to say and is free to say on one's own, one becomes the voice of another. That is the dimension of language that Barth called the word of God.

From this it follows that Barth's conception of Protestant preaching can no more be fit into the classical Protestant conception than Einstein's physics into Newton's. The Barthian conception implies that the task of the preacher is not that of conveying a message in the way that an emissary does; it is not that there are, on the one side, the word of God, inscribed in the Bible, and, on the other side, the human word of the preacher. Rather, the most human, fallible speaking done most on one's own, with only its own witness for support, is also simultaneously the speaking of one who is not the human self and who the self is not. One speaks most on one's own, of a truth for which one answers only on one's own, but a truth which is also false— because it is not to be one's own. The necessity and the possibility of so speaking are the truth and the falsehood that cannot be separated in any word that is the word of God. The Barthian exposition could be elaborated by reference to Bultmann's essay "What Sense Does It Make to Speak of God?" in which Bultmann too sets forth this notion of the fusion of self-speaking and God-speaking.[31] But the point would be the same: with this dialectical theology there appears at the very center of a theological field something that overrides the differences between the divine and the human in speech as well as the differences between the theistic and the atheistic conceptions of the world.

That this takes place specifically in the realm of language and understanding brings us back to our observation that the critiques of modernity involve a recalling of the forgotten capacity to understand being. The question that such critiques open is, accordingly, that of the relation between the sign and the signified, a question that might be said to have become almost an obsession with literary deconstructionists but which affects as well an understanding of current Narcissism and religiosity. Both of these latter express the recalling of the self and the divine in such a way that the signifying quality of the embodiment of each is lost to view. They lose sight of the signifying relation between the concrete immanence of the thing which shows the presence and that reality or power which is shown in, by, and through it. Narcissism poses the problem of the relation between the particularity of the person who can say and think "I" and the universality of the I as such; religiosity—or what in older terms would have been called idolatry—raises the same problem about the relation of the symbol that expresses the not-I to the divine as God.

The relation of sign and signified (or symbol and symbolized) as it appears in the case of instantiation—when the words *I* and *God* instantiate the ones they mean—affects our conception of real existence. In this case, existence is conditioned by temporality. The ones meant and named by the instantiating words are present when they are thought and where they are said, and they are present not as separately perceptible things but as realities or powers appearing in the signs that point to them and point them out. This is a conception of real existence that will hardly fit into a scheme in which everything is divided into the perceptual and the conceptual or into the empirical and the rational.

It is a conception of real existence that depends, instead, upon seeing how the capacity of understanding provides the framework for the connection of the whole. For illustration, we can consider the way in which sign and signified are connected in the *intentionality* of a word like *tree* (on the assumption that we are people who understand the English language). Reading or hearing the word *tree* can bring about in our minds the thought of a tree; in that sense, the word makes us think of the thing to which it refers. At the same time, the thought itself has an intentionality because we recognize that the thought of a tree is not the tree itself; the thought may be *of* the thing, but it is not the thing. Indeed, that is the nature of intentionality—the sign is of something while not being that thing. Finally, we can also recognize that an object perceptible through our senses is the same as what is named and meant in the word. Thus, between the word *tree* on one end and the tree-object on the other there is a continuing movement of pointing-toward, or of intentionality. But the framework of this movement is that of understanding, which makes a transition from one kind of sense-perception to another and then back. Both the word *tree* and the tree-object are empirical or sense-perceptible. The word is an acoustic or visual figure that we can hear or see; so is the tree-object. The word *tree* does not look anything like the tree-object; and yet the sense that we understand in the word can be understood to be the same as the reality that we understand in the object. Despite their physical difference in appearance, the linguistic object and the physical object can be understood as bearing the same meaning. In the framework of understanding, the word has the capacity of engendering the thought; the thought has the capacity of clarifying the perception of a physical object; and the object physically perceived has the capacity of being referred back to the word. The circle is closed by intelligible sense data—the linguistic and the nonlinguistic.

This relation of intentionality between a word and thing is, however, somewhat different from the relation contained in cases where the word not only intends but even instantiates the one to which it refers. *Instantiation* means that in the very thinking or saying of the word involved, something is pointed out as its reference. This is different from object-words like *tree*. Understanding the word *tree* does mean knowing to what kind of object it refers; but it does not mean that the word points out any such object on its own. It awakens the thought of the object in one's mind even when there is no such object around. With instantiating words, the matter is different; for when the thought of "I" is awakened in one's mind, one also becomes the one to whom the word refers at that time. Here the process of understanding is at the same time a process of becoming; one becomes an autonomous self in the moment of thinking or saying the word. This is a more intimate connection of sign and signified than in object-words, and it is the reason why Narcissism, which identifies the self completely with its instantiations, and religiosity, which similarly identifies the divine with its instantiations, are more subtle misunderstandings than the objectification of words as things ("reification"). It is also the reason why we have difficulty forming a picture of the process of becoming a self or of the appearing of the divine. But while critiques of modernity may have made clear why the existence and meaning of the self and of the divine are fundamentally misunderstood if they are put as questions about the reality of an immortal soul or of a transcendent supreme being, they have not made clear why Narcissism and religiosity also misunderstand the self and the divine, nor have they provided a clear picture of a process in which the very understanding of the linguistic signs brings about the ones signified by the signs. The process in which we understand the meaning of "I" is the process in which we each become a self-conscious autonomous self; the process in which we understand the meaning of "God" is also a process in which God comes to be as the divine that no one and nothing really is. The instantiating may be carried even further, in view of Heidegger and Barth, so that the whole of our language, when we understand what we are doing in it, is a double instantiation of the self as I and the divine as God. In either case, however, whether as single words or as a whole manner of speaking, the coming to be of self and the divine is a temporal process because it happens "when" one understands. This temporality is the mode of being of the realities or powers instantiated through language. What picture can we form of that process? If a tree is cut down and turned into a log cabin, the tree no longer exists but the cabin does so. What turns the tree into the cabin is the activity of the cutter and builder. We can easily enough form a picture of that process. Again, a seed may be planted and out of it a tree may grow. The seed no longer exists; the tree does. We can also form a picture of that kind of process. But a person who becomes a self through understanding the word *I* does not cease to exist as a person; the person becomes more than it was— it exists not only as an animated body or embodied consciousness but also as a sign of selfhood. This process is not one of cutting up and putting together—as when one makes a cabin of a tree— nor one of germination and maturity—as in organic growth. The activity of becoming a self is neither constructive nor organic. Rather, it is *creative*, an activity that takes place through the mediation of language and understanding alone. And for that process we do not have familiar pictures. That may be one reason why Bultmann's translation of the concept of faith into the concept of authentic self-understanding, an understanding that brings about selfhood, was and is so widely misunderstood.

Intermediate between the temporality of instantiation and the intentionality of object-language is the *metaphorical process* by which things, while being what they are, can also become signifiers of what they are not. Anything can not only be what it is, a unity of singular and general; it can also bear a meaning that signifies another. Hence, understanding involves not only seeing the sense in signs and being in things but also seeing things as signs either of other senses or of other being. Everything which, in the first place, is a referent of language can become, in turn, a language speaking of something or someone else. Each, by being what it is on its own, can also be a sign of the being of another. Through the metaphorical process, everything can become different; being what it is, it can become at times the bearer of a meaning and reality that it is not.

All of this seems to come, in the end, to the summary statement that what is at issue in the critiques of modernity is the problem of understanding—that is, the problem of recovering the ability not only to ascertain things and to respect persons but also to read signs and then to interpret what we read. Perhaps the difficulty of doing so is perennial. In that case, the anonymity and historicity that are hallmarks of the modern are but a recent version of an ancient spiritual struggle.

Notes

[1]Oswald Spengler, *The Decline of the West* (New York: Knopf, 1932). The literature on modernism is large. Here I list only the following (besides the works cited elsewhere in the notes): Peter Berger, *The Homeless Mind: Modernization and Consciousness* (New York: Random House, 1973) and "Toward a Critique of Modernity," in his *Facing Up to Modernity: Excursions in Society, Politics, and Religion* (New York: Basic Books, 1977), pp. 70–80; Christopher Lasch, *The Culture of Narcissism: American Life in an Age of Diminishing Expectation* (New York: Norton, 1979) and "The Degradation of Work and the Apotheosis of Art: A Humanist Call to Arms," *Harper's*, February 1984, pp. 40–45; Eugen Rosenstock-Huessy, *The Christian Future, or the Modern Mind Outrun* (New York: Harper Torchbook, 1966); Theodor Steinbüchel, "Der Aufbruch einer neuen Zeit," in his *Christliches Mittelalter* (Darmstadt: Wissenschaftliche Buchgesellschaft, 1968), pp. 297–320; Ernst Troeltsch, "Das Wesen des modernen Geistes," *Gesammelte Schriften*, vol. 4, *Aufsätze zur Geistesgeschichte und Religionssoziologie*, ed. Hans Baron (Tübingen: J. C. B. Mohr [Paul Siebeck], 1925), pp. 297–338; and Gabriel Vahanian, *Wait without Idols* (New York: Seabury, 1977).

[2]Jacques Ellul, *The New Demons*, trans. E. Edward Hopkin (New York: Seabury, 1975); quoted according to the excerpts published as "Coda for Christians," *Katallagete—Be Reconciled* 5 (Fall 1975):35.

[3]Martin Heidegger, *Die Grundbegriffe der Metaphysik: Welt—Endlichkeit—Einsamkeit, Gesamtausgabe*, vol. 29/30 (Frankfurt am Main: Vittorio Klostermann, 1983), pp. 117–249.

[4]Aleksandr Solzhenitsyn, *A World Split Apart* (New York: Harper & Row, 1978), p. 47.

[5]George Santayana, *Winds of Doctrine: Studies in Contemporary Opinion* (New York: Scribners, 1913), pp. 56–57.

[6]Ibid., p. 53.

[7]Martin Buber, "What Is Man?" in *Between Man and Man*, trans. Maurice Friedman (New York: Harper & Row, 1938), p. 129; quoting Groethuysen.

[8]Ibid.

[9]Ibid., p. 133.

[10]Martin Heidegger, "Die Zeit des Weltbildes," in his *Holzwege* (Frankfurt am Main: Vittorio Klostermann, 1950), p. 87.

[11]René Descartes, *Meditations on First Philosophy*, in *Philosophers Speak for Themselves: From Descartes to Locke*, ed. T. V. Smith and Marjorie Grene (Chicago: Univ. of Chicago Press, Phoenix Books, 1957), p. 63.

[12]Paul Tillich, "Die technische Stadt als Symbol," *Gesammelte Werke*, ed. Renate Albrecht (Stuttgart: Evangelisches Verlagswerk, 1967), 9:308.

[13]Ibid., p. 310.

[14]Karl Barth, *Anselm: Fides quaerens intellectum*, trans. Ian W. Robertson (Richmond: John Knox Press, 1960).

[15]Friedrich Gogarten, *Der Mensch zwischen Gott und Welt* (Stuttgart: Friedrich Vorwerk, 1956).

[16]Thomas J. J. Altizer, *Total Presence: The Language of Jesus and the Language of Today* (New York: Seabury, 1980).

[17]Alexander Koyré, *From the Closed World to the Infinite Universe* (Baltimore: Johns Hopkins Univ. Press, 1957).

[18]Huston Smith, *Forgotten Truth: The Primordial Tradition* (New York: Harper & Row, 1976); idem, *Beyond the Post-Modern Mind* (New York: Crossroad, 1982).

[19]*Beyond*, p. 134.

[20]Ibid., p. 135.

[21]Ibid., p. 141.

[22]Ibid., pp. 141–42.

[23]Ibid., p. 135.

[24]Ibid., p. 136.

[25]Ibid., p. 138.

[26]Ibid., p. 139.

[27]Fritjof Capra, *The Tao of Physics* (Boulder, Col.: Shambala, 1975).

[8]Martin Heidegger, *Being and Time*, trans. John Macquarrie and Edward Robinson (New York: Harper & Row, 1962).

[29]English translation by Douglas Horton in *The Word of God and the Word of Man* (London: Hodder & Stoughton, 1928), pp. 183–217.

[30]Julian N. Hartt, *A Christian Critique of American Culture* (New York: Harper & Row, 1967), p. 327.

[31]Rudolf Bultmann, "Welchen Sinn hat es, von Gott zu reden?" in his *Faith and Understanding*, trans. Louise Pettibone Smith (New York: Harper & Row, 1969).

Virginia Lectures on Individual and Society

The Committee on Comparative Study of Individual and Society and the Center for Advanced Studies, University of Virginia, together sponsor the biennial Virginia Lectures intended to deepen understanding of the vital issues embedded in the interrelationships between the individual and society in diverse contexts. This volume brings together the fourth Virginia Lectures, delivered in the spring of 1984.